GET
Grounded

Understanding the Historical and
Cultural Context of the Bible

Jennifer Hayes Yates

Edited by Wanda Rogers Hayes

Formatted by Jen Henderson at Wild Words Formatting

jenniferhyates.com

TABLE OF
Contents

The Old Testament

The New Testament

Introduction

For years I approached the Bible as a spiritual horoscope, reading just the verses highlighted in a daily devotional or the parts that spoke to me—seeking answers, encouragement, and direction—but I rarely read through all of the Bible because some of it was confusing or didn't seem to speak to my particular situation.

So, I would read the parts I was comfortable with while avoiding the rest. I read Psalms and Proverbs until they were practically memorized. I knew the Gospels intimately and could quote from Paul's letters. But eventually, I realized I wasn't getting the whole story. You see, we tend to avoid what we don't understand. And some parts of the Bible can be confusing.

It's not all chronological, some things are repeated in different books, the names and places are foreign to us, and we don't always understand cultural differences. All these things make parts of the Bible somewhat challenging to understand and apply to our own lives.

Even after years of sitting through Sunday school classes and Bible studies, I still only understood the Bible in terms of isolated stories. I could tell you about David and Goliath or Ruth or Esther, but I couldn't tell you how their stories connected or, more importantly, how they pointed to the gospel. I read the Old Testament as a historical account, which much of it is, but I never understood how it fit into world history or why that was important to my faith. And to be honest, I didn't understand much of the prophetic books of the Old Testament at all. Most of the laws and prophecies seemed irrelevant to my actual day-to-day life.

But after many years of studying the *whole* Bible, teaching world history, and taking seminary courses, I have learned how all the parts of the Bible fit together to tell one big story, which we call the metanarrative. And every book, chapter, and verse is an important part of that story. Without that whole context, we miss out on valuable meaning in our lives.

The order of our English Bible is not chronological and is sometimes confusing to understand. When we learn the historical, chronological, and cultural context, it makes it easier to interpret what the Bible is communicating. It's also composed of many different categories or genres of literature that we don't interpret in the same way, such as historical narrative, poetry, wisdom literature, prophecy, and letters. The writers use many literary devices, such as parables, metaphors, and hyperbole. Having taught high school English for years, I will explain how these work and how we can interpret the Bible in light of its literary context.

The Bible is all connected. For instance, Hebrews only makes sense in light of Exodus; Galatians needs the background of Genesis. When we understand the Scriptures as a whole, we have a better framework for interpretation and application. We grow our confidence so we can share the truth with others. And we mature in our faith so we can walk out the principles we learn.

> *"For whatever was written in former days was written for our instruction, that through endurance and through the encouragement of the Scriptures we might have hope" (Romans 15:4).*

Understanding the context of the Bible is vital for interpreting and applying it well. As followers of Christ, we are called to be disciples, meaning students or learners. And we are admonished in Scripture to do that well.

> *"Do your best to present yourself to God as one approved, a worker who has no need to be ashamed, rightly handling the word of truth" (2 Timothy 2:15).*

But here's the thing: You don't have to be a scholar or seminary graduate to read and understand the Bible. None of Jesus' apostles were religious scholars, yet they were chosen by Jesus and entrusted with the gospel. I love the account in Acts 4 when Peter and John were arrested for preaching the gospel, then interrogated by the elders and teachers of the law. Peter, empowered by the Holy Spirit, responded to their accusations with grace and truth. Then the text reads:

> *"Now when they saw the boldness of Peter and John, and perceived that they were uneducated, common men, they were astonished. And they recognized that they had been with Jesus" (Acts 4:13).*

Peter and John were fishermen, not scholars. It seems the important qualification was that they had been with Jesus. How does that translate into our time and culture? If we want to have a spiritual impact on those around us, we have to spend time with Jesus. We do that through engaging with His Word. The Bible reveals Him to us and tells us what He is like. So, let's bring balance and clarity to how we approach the Scriptures.

We don't need a seminary degree, but we should make every effort to learn and grow our understanding of God's Word. And we have more resources available to us today than any generation in history. My desire is for this book to be one of those resources that helps you understand the historical and cultural context of God's Word, which is essential to gaining meaning for our lives. As you learn how all the Bible fits together, you will gain valuable knowledge that will increase your understanding of the Bible for your life and fuel your passion for sharing the gospel with others.

God's Word is the inerrant, Spirit-breathed, life-giving gift to us so that we may know Him more and love Him better. Let's be diligent to learn and grow so that we might be grounded in truth and grow our faith.

"Your testimonies are wonderful; therefore my soul keeps them. The unfolding of your words gives light; it imparts understanding to the simple. I open my mouth and pant, because I long for your commandments. Turn to me and be gracious to me, as is your way with those who love your name."

PSALM 119:129-132

Bible Timeline

This timeline will help you see how the people and events of the Bible fit together chronologically.

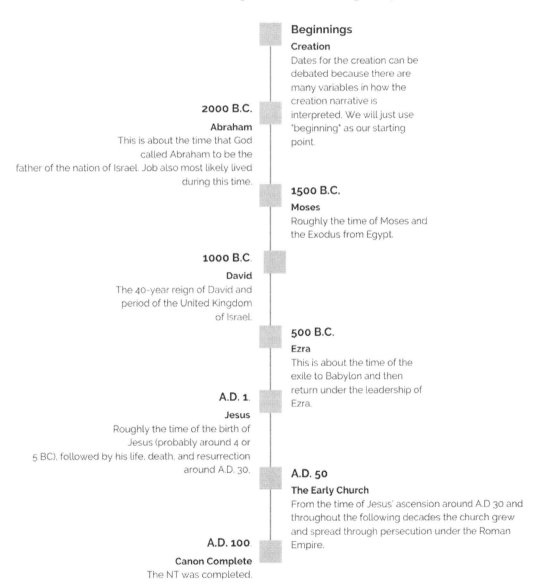

Beginnings

Creation
Dates for the creation can be debated because there are many variables in how the creation narrative is interpreted. We will just use "beginning" as our starting point.

2000 B.C.

Abraham
This is about the time that God called Abraham to be the father of the nation of Israel. Job also most likely lived during this time.

1500 B.C.

Moses
Roughly the time of Moses and the Exodus from Egypt.

1000 B.C.

David
The 40-year reign of David and period of the United Kingdom of Israel.

500 B.C.

Ezra
This is about the time of the exile to Babylon and then return under the leadership of Ezra.

A.D. 1.

Jesus
Roughly the time of the birth of Jesus (probably around 4 or 5 BC), followed by his life, death, and resurrection around A.D. 30.

A.D. 50

The Early Church
From the time of Jesus' ascension around A.D 30 and throughout the following decades the church grew and spread through persecution under the Roman Empire.

A.D. 100.

Canon Complete
The NT was completed.

UNDERSTANDING
Genre

Genre is the category used to describe a work of literature. The Bible is made up of several different genres of literature which determine how we read and interpret. Knowing the genre helps us understand how a book of the Bible should be approached.

The Pentateuch

The first five books of the Bible; historical and theological narrative that sets the foundation for the rest of the Bible, including the metanarrative, which is the overall storyline of the Bible (Creation, the Fall, Redemption, and Restoration) into which the remainder of the Bible fits

We read it as history, while also looking for theological truths as well as the key elements of the metanarrative.

Historical-Theological Narrative

History in the form of stories that include real-life characters, events, actions, and settings, while also conveying theological truths

We read narratives, paying attention to details of context, such as the chronological, historical, and cultural backgrounds, author, audience, and theological themes.

Wisdom and Poetic Literature

A specific genre of ancient Near East literature intended to teach wisdom

Wisdom literature includes proverbs in the form of short, pithy statements read as principles or guidelines for right living. The poetic books use imagery and figurative language, such as parallelism, metaphor, similes, and hyperbole. We approach poetry as something that stirs the emotions, invokes the senses, and inspires on a personal level.

Prophecy

A special type of writing in which prophets sometimes used poetry, oracles, imagery, and symbolism to communicate a message from God.

The prophets called God's people to repentance, to remembrance, and to right living in light of God's covenant and His faithful love. The message often included predictions of things to come. It helps to know the audience to whom the prophet spoke and the historical context of the prophecy.

Epistles

Letters in the New Testament from church leaders to churches or individuals

We approach the epistles as we would read a letter today, reading the text from beginning to end, taking note of the author, the recipient, and the historical and cultural context.

BOOKS OF THE BIBLE
by Genre

1	2	3	4	5
The Pentateuch	Historical–Theological Narrative	Wisdom and Poetic	Prophetic	Epistles
Genesis	Joshua	Job	Isaiah	Romans
Exodus	Judges	Psalms	Jeremiah	1 & 2 Corinthians
Leviticus	Ruth	Proverbs	Lamentations	Galatians
Numbers	1 & 2 Samuel	Ecclesiastes	Ezekiel	Ephesians
Deuteronomy	1 & 2 Kings	Song of Solomon	Daniel	Philippians
	1 & 2 Chronicles		Hosea	Colossians
	Ezra		Joel	1 & 2 Thess.
	Nehemiah		Amos	1 & 2 Timothy
	Esther		Obadiah	Titus
	Matthew		Jonah	Philemon
	Mark		Micah	Hebrews
	Luke		Nahum	James
	John		Habakkuk	1 & 2 Peter
	Acts		Zephaniah	1, 2 & 3 John
			Haggai	Jude
			Zechariah	
			Malachi	
			Revelation	

THE
Metanarrative

The Bible is an amazing, supernatural work made up of 66 books: 39 Old Testament books originally written in Hebrew and 27 New Testament books originally written in Greek. Its writing spans 2000 years with over 40 human authors, yet the entire Word is breathed out by God as He spoke through these human agents to convey His message exactly as He wanted it to be.

> *"All Scripture is God-breathed and is useful for teaching, rebuking, correcting, and training in righteousness so that the man of God may be thoroughly equipped for every good work" (2 Timothy 3:16).*

> *"Above all, you must understand that no prophecy of Scripture came about by the prophet's own interpretation. For prophecy never had its origin in the will of man, but men spoke from God as they were carried along by the Holy Spirit" (2 Peter 1:20-21).*

Only through the divine inspiration of God could 31,102 verses written over 2,000 years tell one consistent story. The metanarrative of Scripture—the name scholars give to the big, overall story—is the account of the creation, the rebellion, the redemption, and the restoration of the world and the people in it. All of Scripture fits into this framework of the metanarrative.

And that story revolves around Jesus Christ of Nazareth, a historical man who is also the divine Son of God. Through historical accounts, poetry, wisdom literature, prophecy, and letters, the Bible points us to the truth of how we got here, how sin came into the world separating us from our Creator, and His plan for the redemption of mankind and the ultimate restoration of all things.

Jesus Himself said that all the Scriptures were about Him.

> *"And beginning with Moses and all the Prophets, he explained to them what was said in all the Scriptures concerning himself" (Luke 24:27, italics mine).*

"He said to them, 'This is what I told you while I was still with you: Everything must be fulfilled that is written about me in the Law of Moses, the Prophets, and the Psalms'" (Luke 24:44, italics mine).

So, as we journey from Genesis to Revelation, we will look for the gospel in every book and see how all the Scriptures are about Jesus. We will learn the historical, chronological, cultural, literary, and biblical context of the Bible. We will identify key principles, different genres, and elements of the metanarrative. And you will get grounded in the truths of Scripture that help grow your faith.

It's a tale for the ages and yet a true story with life-or-death consequences. No ancient writing has more closely documented evidence of historicity. The Bible is not just a good book—it's a powerful, living, active, transformational document that we would do well to study, search, and seek to follow.

Pentateuch: Genesis-Deuteronomy

- Also called the Books of Moses, the Law, or the Torah

- **Timeline:** From Creation to about 1400 BC

- Genesis: Creation, Fall, Judgment, Covenant, Promise

- Exodus: Slavery in Egypt, Freedom, Law, Covenant

- Leviticus: Holiness, Ritual, Relationship

- Numbers: Failure, Consequences

- Deuteronomy: Law and Land

Historical/Theological Narrative: Joshua-Esther

- **Timeline:** 1400 BC-500 BC

- Period of Judges: 1400-1150, cycles of sin, repentance, and rescue

- Period of the United Kingdom of Israel: 1150-970, Saul, David, Solomon

- Period of the Divided Kingdom of Israel: 970-586

- Northern Kingdom (Israel) conquered by the Assyrian Empire in 722

- Southern Kingdom (Judah) conquered by the Babylonian Empire in 586

- The Return: Jews were allowed to return and rebuild under the Persian Empire c. 530-420

Wisdom and Poetic Books: Job-Song of Solomon

- **Timeline:** varies, Job is the earliest, Psalms vary with different authors from different periods, Proverbs, Ecclesiastes, and Song of Solomon during the time of Solomon (900s)

- Job: suffering and perseverance

- Psalms: worship

- Proverbs: wisdom

- Ecclesiastes: philosophy

- Song of Solomon: love and marriage

Prophets: Isaiah-Malachi

- Pre-exile: 700s-mid 500s, Hosea, Amos, Jonah, Nahum, Obadiah, Habakkuk, Isaiah, Jeremiah, Joel, Micah, Zephaniah, and Lamentations

- Exile: 600s-500s, Ezekiel, Daniel

- Post-exile: 500s-400s, Haggai, Zechariah, Malachi

The Intertestamental Period: 400 years between the testaments

- Persia (559-331) Cyrus allowed Israel to rebuild and restore worship

- Greece (331-164) Allowed Judah free rule, Sanhedrin formed, common Greek language

- Jewish Independence (164-63) Maccabean revolt, self-rule, returned to God, leaders declined

- Rome (63-AD 165) Established peace, roads, and commerce; used the Greek language

The Gospels: Matthew-John

- Life of Christ from different perspectives
- **Timeline:** 5-4 BC-AD 30s
- Matthew: Jesus as Son of David, Kingly Messiah
- Mark: Jesus as the suffering Son of Man
- Luke: Jesus as the compassionate Savior of the world
- John: Jesus as the Son of God, the Word made flesh

Historical/Theological Narrative: Acts

- **Timeline:** about AD 30-60
- Historical account of the early church

The Pauline Epistles: Romans-Philemon

- **Timeline:** about 50-60
- Romans: salvation, faith, grace
- 1 and 2 Corinthians: addressed divisions, immorality, and deceivers in the church
- Galatians: warning against legalism and defense of justification by faith
- Ephesians: what it means to follow Christ
- Philippians: joy, the humility of Jesus, encouragement
- Colossians: warning against false teaching and encouragement to grow
- 1 and 2 Thessalonians: teaching on Christ's return
- 1 and 2 Timothy: encouraged Timothy to stand against false teaching and be faithful in ministry
- Titus: encouragement toward good works
- Philemon: Paul appeals to a brother to forgive his runaway slave

The General Epistles: Hebrews-Jude

- **Timeline:** late 40s to late 90s

- Hebrews: the supremacy of Christ over the old covenant

- James: encouragement to put faith in action

- 1 and 2 Peter: call to holiness; warning against false teachers

- 1, 2, and 3 John: emphasized love and obedience; warning against heresy; 3 John is written to an individual to praise him

- Jude: warning against heresy

Prophecy: The Revelation

- **Timeline:** late 90s

- Prophecy

- Symbolism

- Final judgment and reign of King Jesus

The Old

Testament

"The unfolding of your words gives light...."
Psalm 119:130a

The Pentateuch

Foundation

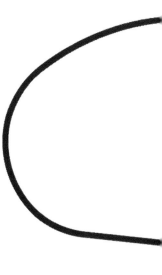

THE
Pentateuch

The first five books of the Bible are called the Pentateuch, a Greek term meaning "five scrolls." Believed to be written by Moses, they are also called the Law of Moses or the Torah, the Jewish term meaning "teaching." They are historical narratives with theological implications. We read them as historical accounts involving people, places, and events, while also looking for theological principles. These first five books set the foundation for the rest of the Bible. God established the concepts of the Creation of the world, the Fall of man, judgment for sin, covenant, the promise of redemption and future restoration, the law, freedom, holiness, relationship, consequences, and hope.

The metanarrative—that overarching story of the whole Bible—starts here in the first five books. In fact, we find the Creation and the Fall of man in the first three chapters, along with the promise of redemption and the hope of the future restoration of all things, culminating in the book of Revelation.

Much of the Bible needs the context of these first five books for full understanding. Galatians needs the context of Genesis. Hebrews needs the context of Exodus and Leviticus. All the prophets point back to the promise of blessings for obedience and curses for disobedience that God established for the Israelites through Moses in Deuteronomy. We need the biblical context of the whole Bible to make sense of its individual books.

The first eleven chapters of Genesis, the account of primeval history, describe the Creation, the Fall, and the proliferation of sin through Cain and Abel, the time of Noah, the tower of Babel, and the call of Abraham. Chapters eleven through fifty, the account of patriarchal history, describe the lives of Abraham and his descendants, the nation of Israel, through whom Jesus descended and came into our world.

GENESIS 1-11

Key Term: Creation

Key People: Adam, Eve, Cain, Abel, Noah

Looking back at the timeline, you will see that Genesis begins with Creation. The word Genesis, *Bereshit* in Hebrew, means "in the beginning." We don't have a specific date for Creation because scholars debate the many variables in how these first few chapters are interpreted. I find it more profitable to understand the theological implications of the Creation account. Genesis answers the questions of who we are and how we got here. It reveals to us the origin story of the universe and mankind. We learn that God is omnipotent, sovereign, and eternal and that everything He created was good.

We find the concept of the Trinity, a word not found in Scripture but revealed through the use of the terms Father, Son, and Holy Spirit to describe the different persons of the divinity. In the Creation account, the Spirit hovers over the water. God says "Let us make man in our image," using the plural pronoun to refer to Himself (Gen. 1:26). Then John tells us in his Gospel that Jesus was there in the beginning (John 1:1, 14).

God created humans in his own image for fellowship with Him, which is where we get our intrinsic value. Then temptation and sin entered the world as Adam and Eve, the first humans, were given a moral choice. Satan in the form of the serpent tempted them and they sinned against God. This gives us the answer to how sin came into the world and why evil and suffering are in the world. We learn that there's judgment for sin. God intended them to live forever in relationship with Him, but sin forever marred that relationship, and the earth was corrupted.

The serpent was cursed, and God made a promise to crush the head of the serpent, a foreshadowing of Jesus' victory over sin and death on the cross. And then God did something very beautiful. Although there were consequences for Adam and Eve's sin, He covered their nakedness and shame with animal skins, which shows us a beautiful picture of blood sacrifice for sin. We see the foundational principles of sin, judgment, and sacrifice in the very beginning of the Bible. We also see that once sin came into the world, it infected the whole human race. Sin perpetuated from one generation to the next as we read of Cain and Abel, and then the time of Noah, when the world became so dark with sin that God destroyed it with a flood, saving only Noah and his family. After the flood, they repopulated the earth. But just a few generations later humanity once again rebelled against God at the Tower of Babel as they attempted to build a tower to God to make a name for themselves. God scattered them throughout the world and confused their language, but God still had a plan to redeem the world to Himself. So, He chose a righteous man, Abraham, through whom He would build a nation that would eventually bring blessing and redemption to the whole world.

GENESIS 12-50

Key Term: Covenant
Key People: Abraham, Sarah, Isaac, Jacob, Joseph

God called Abraham to be in covenant with Him and to be the father of a great nation. The story of Abraham is a beautiful story of God calling a righteous man who lived among idol worshipers, including his own father. God called Abraham to leave his home and follow Him to a land He would show him. Abraham didn't know where he was going, but he took his wife Sarah and his nephew Lot, and he followed God. That faith was credited to him as righteousness. God eventually told Abraham He would make him the father of a great nation and that his descendants would be as many as the sand on the shore and the stars in the sky. Through Abraham, all the nations of the world will be blessed. This Abrahamic Covenant was the promise of God to bring His Son, the Messiah, into the world to redeem the world to Himself. Matthew traces this lineage of Jesus back to Abraham in his gospel account (Matt. 1:1-16).

Abraham was an old man when God made the promise, and his wife Sarah was barren. Abraham and his wife Sarah eventually had Isaac, the child of the promise. One day when Isaac was young, God called Abraham to Mount Moriah to sacrifice his son to Him. The book of Hebrews tells us that Abraham believed and trusted God so much, that he knew that even if he obeyed God and sacrificed his son that God was able to raise him from the dead (Heb. 11:19). He believed the promise and that promise was coming through that child. So they continued up the mountain, but God stopped Abraham from sacrificing his son because it was just a test of Abraham's heart. God provided a ram for the sacrifice, another picture of blood sacrifice being provided by God Himself, pointing to the gospel. God wanted all of Abraham's trust to be in Him. Abraham passed that test, and he is revered throughout the Bible as a great man of faith.

Isaac had a son named Jacob who was a deceiver, yet God redeemed him and changed his name to Israel. He became the father of twelve sons who became the twelve tribes of Israel. One of those sons was Joseph, and Joseph is the one that the story continues through in the book of Genesis. Joseph was hated by his brothers because he was daddy's favorite. They were going to kill him, but they decided to sell him into slavery instead. Joseph ended up in Egypt where God worked providentially through him to save the entire nation of Israel. Because he was a man of integrity and righteousness, he obeyed God and God's hand was on him. God continued to prosper him and situate him in all the right places so that Joseph ended up second in command in all of Egypt. He was able to store up during a famine so that all of his family came to Egypt for food. We see God at work to sustain the nation in a time of famine so that He could keep His covenant with Abraham. What Satan intended for evil in Joseph's life, God used for good so that the whole nation would be saved; because through that nation, Israel, the Messiah would come.

The book of Genesis establishes the foundational themes of Creation, rebellion, covenant, redemption, sacrifice, consequences, and judgment. It presents us with many of the attributes or characteristics of God, such as His faithfulness, lovingkindness, sovereignty, power, and justice, and continually points us forward in history to the coming of Christ who would fulfill the promise of redemption and restoration for all the world.

"So God created man in his own image,
in the image of God he created him;
male and female he created them."

GENESIS 1:27

EXODUS

Key Term: Commandment

Key People: Moses, Aaron, Miriam, Joshua

Exodus begins with all of the Israelites in Egypt because of the famine. They ended up being there for a very long time—about four hundred years altogether—so, the generations had died that were originally there. The Israelites had grown in number, and the current Pharaoh was threatened by them, so they were forced into slave labor.

God called Moses from a burning bush, revealing Himself to Moses as *I am*. It's where we get the name, *Yahweh*. He used Moses to lead the Israelites out of slavery in Egypt through a series of plagues that eventually caused the Pharaoh to let them go. The last plague involved the killing of the firstborn son of all the Egyptians, so God told the Israelites to put the blood of a spotless Lamb over their doorways so that when the Death Angel came, their firstborns would be spared. We see again this picture of blood sacrifice protecting them from death which is what sin leads to. It is a stunning picture of the gospel and the hope of redemption, pointing to Jesus, the spotless Lamb of God. This event marked the beginning of the celebration of Passover by the Jews, commemorating their deliverance from Egypt, slavery, and death.

Exodus means "the way out" in Greek, and it is a story of deliverance and redemption. God's people, whom He had settled in Canaan through Abraham, had been delivered from famine in Canaan and extinction in Egypt. After four hundred years, the place of protection had become a place of oppression, and in His faithfulness, God delivered them from Egypt so they could return to the Promised Land.

As the Israelites continued their journey through the wilderness and back to Canaan, God provided for their every need. He revealed a way for the people to live in relationship with Him by giving them the Ten Commandments. *Commandment* is such an important theme in the book of Exodus. God gave Moses the commandments to show the people His standard of righteousness to be in relationship with Him. From Genesis to Revelation, the Bible consistently reveals God as a personal Being who desires relationship with the individuals He created. The commandments revealed to them their sinful state and their need for a Savior. Yet they failed to keep the commands and constantly rejected God and His ways, turning to idols instead.

God gave Moses instructions for building a tabernacle so He could dwell among them. It was a traveling worship center where sacrifices would take place as atonement for the sins of the people. Once again, we see the idea of sacrifice and blood atoning for sin. Everything in the tabernacle pointed to Jesus, from the Holy Place where the lampstand reminds us that Jesus said, "I am the light of the world" to the table of showbread demonstrating that God was their provider and sustainer. Jesus said in John 8, "I am the bread of life." Here in the Holy Place, in front of the curtain separating the Holy Place from the Most Holy Place was the altar of incense where a sweet-smelling incense would be burned continuously. The incense created a fragrant aroma that filled the Holy Place with a cloud. In Psalm 141, David compared this incense to prayer rising before God. Behind the thick curtain was the Ark of the Covenant, where God's presence dwelled among them at the mercy seat.

The tabernacle was a way for a holy God to dwell among a sinful people. It was a beautiful illustration and foreshadowing of Jesus. You couldn't go behind that curtain unless you were the high priest and then only one day out of the year on the Day of Atonement. The high priest would take the blood of the sacrifice and place it on the altar to atone for the sins of all the people. It was such a marvelous picture of God's holiness and a foreshadowing of Jesus as our Great High Priest and as the sacrifice for sin once and for all (Heb. 4:14-16).

Those sacrifices had to be made every day, but Jesus' sacrifice was the ultimate fulfillment of everything tabernacle worship pointed to. The apostle John would later write, "And the Word became flesh and dwelt among us, and we have seen his glory, glory as of the only Son from the Father, full of grace and truth" (John 1:14). The word translated *dwelt* is literally *tabernacled*. God's desire has always been to dwell among us.

Moses is a type of Christ as the deliverer of God's people from bondage. The title *Christ* is from the Greek *Christos* and corresponds to the Hebrew title *Messiah*, both meaning "the Anointed One." When Scripture portrays a "type" or figure that points to the Christ, we get a glimpse of God's plan of salvation from the beginning. Later, Hebrews presents Jesus as the better one who supersedes the ministry of Moses and brings deliverance from the bondage of sin to all people at all times.

Exodus serves as a reminder to us of God's desire to dwell among us, His faithfulness, His deliverance, His provision, and His protection.

. . . .

"'And let them make me a sanctuary that I may dwell in their midst'."

EXODUS 25:8

. . . .

LEVITICUS

Key Term: Consecration
Key People: The Levites, Moses, Aaron

Remember the twelve tribes of Jacob? Levi was one of those sons, one of the brothers of Joseph. His tribe, the Levites, was the one put in charge of this tabernacle and the instructions for worship. The book of Leviticus outlines those instructions as well as the call to holy living.

Leviticus means "about the Levites." The book of Leviticus moves from the narrative of Genesis and Exodus to the outlining of the rules for holy living and for approaching a holy God. Many people get bogged down in all the regulations of Leviticus because they seem so far removed from our culture today. Yet, they teach us about the holiness of God and how sinful people could be in relationship with Him prior to the sacrifice of Jesus. He set the Israelites apart to be different, a holy people separate from all the nations around them. All the other nations were polytheists, worshiping many gods; Israel was to be different—a monotheistic people who worship Him alone. The offerings and the sacrifices were to show them how to temporarily approach a holy God.

LAWS AND OFFERINGS IN LEVITICUS

RITUAL/ CEREMONIAL LAWS	PRIESTHOOD LAWS	PURITY/ HOLINESS LAWS
Burnt Offerings	Consecration/Ordination of Priests	Clean and Unclean Animals
Grain Offerings	The Day of Atonement	Purification Laws
Peace Offerings	Worship at Tabernacle	Sexual Relationships
Sin Offerings	Holiness for Priests	Love for Neighbor
Guilt Offerings	Unacceptable Sacrifices	Idolatry
Feast Days		Laws about Vows
Sabbath Laws/Jubilee		

Leviticus covers three main types of laws for the Israelites: ritual laws for offerings and special days, priesthood laws for the duties of the Levites, and purity laws for holy living.

Leviticus begins with the ritual laws that cover the five different types of offerings: burnt offerings, grain offerings, peace offerings, sin offerings, and guilt offerings. Some of the offerings were to express thanksgiving and praise; some of the offerings were for the forgiveness of sins. These sacrifices would atone for sin temporarily, teaching them the price for sin and pointing the way to the once-for-all sacrifice that would come through Jesus.

Leviticus outlines the regulations for the priesthood, including instructions for the ordination of priests to carry out the duties of tabernacle worship. Special emphasis was placed on the Day of Atonement already mentioned. This was that special day once a year in which the high priest would be ceremonially cleansed, and then he would sacrifice a goat for the sins of all the people. The blood of the sacrifice would be placed on the mercy seat behind the veil in the Most Holy Place. A second goat, the scapegoat, would be sent into the wilderness, symbolizing the sins of the people being carried away. This special day was to remind the people of the price of sin and to cleanse them from all unholiness.

The third type of laws are the moral or purity laws, like the Ten Commandments, that instructed them in how to relate rightly with God and with others. Within these holiness laws were dietary laws and very practical procedures for cleanliness. Some of them were about how to treat other people, but many of these ritual laws were about consecrating or setting apart the Israelites from the nations around them.

Many people question how Christians should interpret and apply these Scriptures that were written to Israel. As we read the many regulations, we will notice that the law has theological implications that are important for us today. The sin offerings of Leviticus established the principle that all sin has a price. By His sacrifice on the cross, Jesus has provided the means of atonement for sin that the law stipulated through sacrificial worship (Rom. 3:25). Hebrews 8-10 outlines for us the fulfillment of the OT law, which was a "copy and shadow of what is in heaven" (8:5).

The Old Testament law could not save, it could only show what God expected for those in a relationship with Him and point them to a future hope in Christ (Rom. 3:20). "The former regulation is set aside because it was weak and useless (for the law made nothing perfect), and a better hope is introduced, by which we draw near to God" (Heb. 7:19). The law made a way for the Israelites to draw near to God in worship; Jesus has made a way for us to draw near through faith. The law defined holiness and righteousness for the Israelites; Jesus came to show us grace and truth (Gal. 3:24, John 1:17). Without understanding the nature and scope of the Mosaic Law, we lose the impact of the depravity of our sin and our need for a Savior.

Paul went to great lengths in both Galatians and Romans to teach the New Testament church that we are no longer bound by the Mosaic Law (Rom. 3, Gal. 3), but we know that some of the Old Testament law has moral implications that don't change, such as the Ten Commandments. We learn from the ceremonial laws about the holiness of God, the requirement of a blood sacrifice to atone for sin, and the beauty of God's desire to be near His people (Exod. 29:42-43). These Scriptures are valuable for us because they teach us about God.

When it comes to practical application, some have divided the Old Testament law into categories, such as moral, civil, and ceremonial laws, but the Bible does not make those distinctions.[1] Some laws would then fall into more than one category (such as the law against adultery which would be both a moral and a civil law), so those distinctions don't seem to apply.[2] A more consistent approach to the Old Testament law would be to discern what a particular law meant to its original audience and what principle it teaches. Then we should look to see if that principle is reaffirmed in the New Testament, such as the principles of loving God and loving our neighbor.[3]

We are under a new covenant in Christ. So, while the Old Testament law holds a different implication for us today than it did for ancient Israel, it has much value in teaching us about the holiness of God, His desire for relationship, and the power and significance of the gospel. We live under a new covenant through the blood of Christ who calls us to the command, both old (Lev. 19:18) and new: "A new command I give you: love one another. As I have loved you, so you must love one another" (John 13:34).

Leviticus also covers the festivals and holy days that God instructed the Israelites to keep. These were reminders of God's covenant faithfulness and provision for the people. The first four feasts have been fulfilled by Jesus' first coming, as His crucifixion, burial, resurrection, and outpouring of the Holy Spirit took place during those particular feasts. We can be assured the last three will be fulfilled at His second coming.

---

[1] J. Daniel Hays, "Reading the Old Testament Laws" in *Read the Bible for Life: Your Guide to Understanding and Living God's Word*, ed. George H. Guthrie *(Nashville: B&H Publishing, 2011)*, 98.

[2] Hays, "Reading Old Testament," 98.

[3] Ibid., 102.

FEAST	FULFILLMENT
The Passover Feast	Jesus' crucifixion
Feast of Unleavened Bread	Jesus' burial
First Fruits	Jesus' resurrection
Pentecost	The Holy Spirit
Feast of Trumpets	
Day of Atonement	
Feast of Tabernacles	

· ·

"'And I will walk among you and will be your God, and you shall be my people.'"

LEVITICUS 26:12

· ·

NUMBERS

Key Term: Complaining
Key People: Moses, Joshua, Caleb

Numbers begins where Exodus ends. The Israelites had been given the Law at Mt. Sinai and were preparing for their journey to the Promised Land. God numbered the people through a census and then assigned the responsibilities for each tribe moving forward. The Levites were assigned to guard and transport the tabernacle. Numbers is the account of the Israelites and their struggle to trust and obey God. As soon as the journey grew difficult, their trust wavered and they began to complain.

They told Moses they would have been better off back in Egypt where at least they had some leeks and cucumbers. As they complained about the lack of food, God sent them manna. When they got sick of the manna, God gave them quail. When they complained about a lack of water, God gave them water. They lost sight of the fact that He was leading them with a cloud by day and fire by night. His presence was with them continually with the Ark of the Covenant. God blessed them with His presence, provision, and protection as they traveled.

When they arrived at Kadesh Barnea, right outside of Canaan, they were ready to go in and take the land that God had promised—a land flowing with milk and honey. They sent in twelve spies to survey the land and the people. While Joshua and Caleb had faith in God's presence and power to defeat their enemies, the other ten spies came back with a negative report of fear. Because of their doubt and unbelief, the Israelites wandered in the desert for forty more years until that whole generation died out.

God had protected them against their enemies, but they didn't trust that He would continue to be with them. Joshua and Caleb were the only ones of their generation to trust God's character and His promises and to eventually take possession of the land. As the Israelites continued their journey, the complaining continued and Moses became exasperated with the Israelites. Because he only partially obeyed God's instruction, he also was unable to enter the Promised Land. Numbers ends with Moses giving instructions to this new generation who was about to take possession of the land, the inheritance of the people of God.

Numbers teaches us to be grateful for God's provision and protection, to trust His faithfulness to us, and to believe in His love and care for us despite our failures. It also points us to our hope in Jesus to change our rebellious hearts and empower us to live faithfully.

"'The LORD bless you and keep you; the LORD make his face to shine upon you and be gracious to you; the LORD lift up his countenance upon you and give you peace.'"

NUMBERS 6:24-26

DEUTERONOMY

Key Term: Commitment
Key People: Moses, Joshua

Deuteronomy means "second law" because Moses reviewed the Law and the covenant before this second generation moved forward to take over Canaan. He reminded them of the long journey that they had been on. These were the descendants of those who left Egypt. Moses called them to renew their covenant with God so they could go into this new land and be what God had called them to be. He reminded them that God's covenant with them was conditional.

God had chosen them to be His special possession. He had delivered them from bondage in Egypt and was giving them an abundant land. Moses encouraged the people to respond to God's faithfulness with trust and obedience. He reminded them that God is a promise keeper. He is the all-powerful, sovereign, and faithful God who led them through the wilderness and provided for their every need. He continued to bless them despite their rebellion because God would keep His promise to Abraham.

Moses encouraged Israel to conquer the inhabitants and take possession of the land God had promised. He stressed God's law and reminded them of the blessings of obedience and the curse of disobedience. He called upon Israel to renew their commitment to the covenant and to enter Canaan with their hearts devoted to God.

Deuteronomy is the foundation of the rest of the Old Testament. Quoted more than any other OT book, including by Jesus, it is a call to faithfulness and obedience. As Israel's story continues in the historical books of the OT, we will see that their failure to obey God's law led to the curses promised in Deuteronomy 28. The writers of the historical and prophetic books often allude to these foundational truths in Deuteronomy because they explain the path that Israel took.

Because the nation turned away from God to worship idols, they ended up destroyed, taken captive, and exiled to a foreign land.

Deuteronomy teaches us God's faithfulness, justice, love, patience, and call to righteousness. It serves as a reminder for believers today of the blessings of our inheritance awaiting us in heaven and of the peace and joy that come from walking in obedience.

"'Hear, O Israel: The LORD our God, the LORD is one.'"

DEUTERONOMY 6:1

The Historical Books

Israel

THE HISTORICAL
Books

The books of Joshua through Esther are called Historical books because they narrate the history of the nation of Israel. In these books, we see how the people of God sometimes did, but often did *not,* keep the foundational things established in the first five books. Just as with any historical narrative, we see the truth of how people lived—the good, the bad, and the ugly. So, not all of what we read in these books is *prescribing* the behaviors God desires of us; rather, they are *describing* the behaviors of a particular people at a particular time in history.

What we do learn is what God desires of His people. We see the consequences of their sin when they rebelled against Him, and we see the blessings they experienced when they walked in obedience. And we learn more about God's character. He is a faithful God who keeps His promises and who continued to offer love, mercy, and hope to a people who continually rejected Him.

This timeline demonstrates the historical period covered by these narratives and helps situate the books in their historical and chronological context.

TIMELINE OF THE HISTORICAL NARRATIVES

APPROXIMATE DATE	HISTORICAL PERIOD
1440-1150 BC	Period of the Judges
1150-970 BC	The United Kingdom
970-586 BC	The Divided Kingdom
722 BC	Fall of the Northern Kingdom of Israel to Assyria
586 BC	Fall of the Southern Kingdom of Judah to Babylon
530-420 BC	Period of the Return from Exile

JOSHUA

Key Term: Conquest
Key People: Joshua, Caleb, Rahab

This book is about Israel under the leadership of Joshua as he took over after Moses' death. Joshua led the people into Canaan, the Promised Land of the Covenant, but they had to conquer the people who lived there first. These people, the Canaanites, were morally depraved and wicked, engaging in child sacrifice to their gods (Lev. 18:21, Deut. 12:31). The book begins with God commissioning Joshua to lead the people as they prepared for the battle to take Jericho, the first fortified city they approached in Canaan.

Joshua sent spies into Jericho first, where they encountered Rahab, a prostitute and probably an innkeeper. She helped the spies by hiding them from the men of Jericho and sharing vital information with them. She had heard how their God led them out of Egypt and gave them victory against their enemies, and she acknowledged He was the one true God. In return, the spies agreed to save her and her family during the battle. The Battle of Jericho was a supernatural event in which God demonstrated that He alone would be glorified. Rahab and her family were saved because of their faith in Israel's God, and they became assimilated into the nation of Israel. She later married Salmon, the father of Boaz, and became a part of the lineage of David and of Christ (Matt. 15).

Israel crossed the Jordan and took possession of the land as God drove out the nations before them. He alone was responsible for their victories. As they consecrated themselves and followed Him, God continued to lead them. When one man, Achan, failed to obey God's commands, the whole nation suffered defeat at the hands of their enemy. The sin of one man caused suffering for many, and we see the principle of just how destructive sin is, not just personally and morally, but even socially.

Once this sin was exposed, God continued to lead Joshua in taking the city, and Joshua responded by renewing the covenant between the people and God. Israel continued to follow God in conquering the immoral people of Canaan and taking possession of the land God promised, but they failed to drive out all the inhabitants of the land as God had said. The gods of those people would eventually become a snare to them, just as God had warned.

God gave Joshua instructions for how the land should be divided among the tribes except for the Levites, who were set apart as the priesthood to care for the Tabernacle. They were not given their own land but cities within the land of the other tribes. Then Joshua gave a last farewell speech in which he called upon Israel to again renew their commitment to the covenant by choosing to serve God as their Lord and the people agreed to follow God.

Joshua is an exciting historical account of the nation of Israel, and it has much to teach us today. It serves as a reminder of God's standard of righteousness, His faithfulness, and His supernatural power to act on behalf of His people.

"'This book of the Law shall not depart from your mouth, but you shall meditate on it day and night so that you may be careful to do according to all that is written in it. For then you will make your way prosperous, and then you will have good success. Have I not commanded you? Be strong and courageous. Do not be frightened, and do not be dismayed, for the LORD your God is with you wherever you go.'"

JOSHUA 1:8-9

JUDGES

Key Term: Corruption
Key People: Deborah, Gideon, Samson

Despite the Israelites' insistence that they would serve and obey God (Josh. 24:24), they fell into a cycle of apostasy (turning away from God), oppression by their enemies, supplication to God for help, and deliverance through someone God raised up for His purposes. These leaders were called judges, which was a term referring to their leadership and authority.

After the Joshua generation died out, the new generation "did not know the LORD or the work that he had done for Israel" (Judg. 2:10b). The Israelites had failed to drive out all the inhabitants of Canaan as God had instructed, and the gods of those people became a snare to them. As they plunged deeper into immorality, the book of Judges describes gruesome details of bloodshed, rape, and disgrace.

The book of Judges can be characterized by the very last verse in the book: "In those days there was no king in Israel. Everyone did what was right in his own eyes" (Judges 21:25). The period of the judges is the time between Joshua and the monarchy. It was a very dark time in the history of Israel as they repeated this cycle of corruption and moral failure, judgment for their sin at the hands of their enemies, and deliverance via a judge God would send in answer to their cries for help. They would be restored to God and have peace for a few years, and then they would fall back into sin and rebellion against God. This cycle was repeated several times in the book of Judges.

This is a period of theocracy because God was their King as He ruled Israel through these judges. When they rebelled, God heard their cries of repentance and delivered them from oppression. He is the faithful covenant God, showing mercy and deliverance despite their sin, pointing to the hope that is to come in Jesus. The judges get that name because some of them settled disputes among the people as an arbiter or judiciary. Deborah was one of those, the only female judge in Israel's history. Others were military leaders, such as Gideon and Samson.

The book of Judges is full of warfare, bloodshed, death, and depravity. This period in Israel's history shows the result of rebellion against God and His commands. When they did what was right in their own eyes rather than what God revealed as right through His law, they served the gods of the nations around them. An oft-repeated phrase in Judges is "…the people of Israel did what was evil in the sight of the LORD and served the Baals. And they abandoned the LORD, the God of their fathers, who had brought them out of the land of Egypt" (Judges 2:11-12).

Despite their sin, God was faithful to bring deliverance and hope. Even though He would use these judges, speak through them, and guide them in military battles, He used very supernatural means for them to win these battles. So we see God's hand at work as He not only redeemed his people and called them back to Himself but did it in a way that revealed His power and glory and left little room for their own. God showed them continually that he was the one saving them. He demonstrated His heart for His people and the hope of redemption during this morally depraved time in Israel's history.

The book of Judges teaches us of the depth of sin to which people can fall and the need for a Savior. It also shows us the love and mercy of God, who continues to hear and respond to the cries of His people.

. . . .

*"Whenever the LORD raised up
judges for them, the LORD was with the
judge, and he saved them from the hand
of their enemies all the days of the judge.
For the LORD was moved to pity by their
groaning because of those who afflicted
and oppressed them."*

JUDGES 2:18

. . . .

RUTH

Key Term: Contrast

Key People: Ruth, Naomi, Boaz

The book of Ruth is a stunning historical narrative of devotion, redemption, and hope amid apostasy, darkness, and depravity. Set in the period of the judges, Ruth is a shining example of faithfulness in stark contrast to the Israelites' moral decline following the death of Joshua. Against this dark background, the book of Ruth begins with "In the days when the judges ruled, there was a famine in the land…" (Ruth 1:1a). Using brilliant story-telling and dialogue, the unknown writer of Ruth penned this short account, sometime after David's reign, to possibly legitimize David's kingship. Ruth's brevity, however, does not diminish its significance for developing important theology, such as the inclusiveness of the gospel, the blessings of obedience, and the idea of redemption.

In contrast to Judges, which describes the sinfulness of this period, Ruth shares that a faithful remnant still existed. Ironically, famine came to Bethlehem, which means "house of bread," possibly as judgment on the immorality and apostasy of Judah. A man named Elimelech and his family traveled to Moab for food, reminding us of Israel's relocation to Egypt under similar conditions. Elimelech's sons married Moabite women. While marriage to Moabites was not forbidden in the law (as it was to Canaanites), Moabites were excluded from worship (Deut. 23:3), so their marriage to foreigners was still significant. Moab was still an enemy of Israel, although the text never mentions it. First, Moab was the son of Lot and his own daughter following a drunken, incestuous relationship (Gen. 19:37). Second, the Moabites were excluded from worship for two reasons: They refused to offer sustenance to the Israelites when they left Egypt, and they had hired Balaam to curse the Israelites (Deut. 23:4). Yet, in this story, Ruth the Moabitess was the example of loyalty, devotion, and loving-kindness that was missing among the Israelites in the book of Judges.

God used a foreigner to contrast with the depth of immorality of His people whom He called and set apart as a nation unto Him. Two aspects of theology are seen here. First, the covenant with Abraham was that all the nations would be blessed through him and his descendants (Genesis 12:3), so there is a foreshadowing in Ruth that the gospel would be for all people, not just the Israelites. And second, God looks at the heart. The 1984 *NIV Study Bible*'s introduction to Ruth says it so beautifully: "She strikingly exemplifies the truth that participation in the coming kingdom of God is decided, not by blood or birth, but by the conformity of one's life to the will of God through the 'obedience that comes from faith' (Rom. 1:5)." This emphasis is seen in the life of Rahab as well. Both of these foreign women put their faith in the God of Israel and were saved. Daniel Block states: "This

Moabite serves as a model for all ethnic non-Israelites: if they will cast their lot in with the people of Israel and commit themselves to Yahweh their God, they too may find a home in the covenant community."[4]

The narrative conclusion is significant because it shows the contrast between Naomi's emptiness and fullness, highlighting the blessings of obedience. After Elimelech and both his sons had died, his distraught widow Naomi discovered the famine was over and decided to return to Bethlehem, urging both daughters-in-law to stay with their families. Orpah went home, but Ruth declared her loyalty to Naomi and the God of Israel (1:16-17). In Bethlehem the women were without husbands to provide, so Ruth gleaned behind the barley harvesters, a provision in the law for the poor (Lev. 19:9-10). There she met Boaz, who protected and provided for her, ultimately becoming her kinsman redeemer so that Elimelech's family line would be continued and Naomi's life made full again.

At the conclusion of the narrative, the son born to Ruth was identified as the grandfather of King David, pointing to the line of Christ. Boaz's role as a kinsman redeemer is significant as a type of Christ. The idea of a kinsman-redeemer was taken from commands in the law that instructed family members to redeem land or persons that had been sold outside the family due to poverty (Lev. 25:25-28, 47-49). The levirate marriage was a provision in Deuteronomy 25:5-10 that allowed a widow to marry her brother-in-law to continue her husband's family line. Both of these laws seem to be the spirit behind the idea of a kinsman-redeemer in Ruth. As God worked behind the scenes of this story, He orchestrated events in such a way that Boaz, like Christ, showed favor and grace to a foreigner outside the law, destitute, with no hope for the future, and he did so based solely on her faith. Ruth left behind her life in a pagan culture to seek a new life among the people of Naomi's God, and her faith was rewarded. Not only did a birth figure prominently in the good news, but that ancestral line led to King David, another type of Christ, and ultimately to Jesus Himself.

Ruth is a masterpiece of drama, dialogue, and intrigue, yet it is as theologically rich as it is literarily so. The contrast between the apostasy of the time and the faith of Ruth, the ancestors of Ruth and Boaz compared with their descendants, and the typological significance of Boaz as a kinsman redeemer all function together in a story of redemption, a microcosm of the gospel itself in which the main character is God.

---

[4] Daniel Isaac Block, Judges, Ruth, vol. 6, *The New American Commentary* (Nashville: Broadman & Holman Publishers, 1999), 598.

"'The Lord repay you for what you have done, and a full reward be given you by the Lord, the God of Israel, under whose wings you have come to take refuge!'"

RUTH 2:12

1 AND 2 SAMUEL

Key Term: Calling
Key People: Samuel, Saul, David

1 and 2 Samuel were originally one book that narrates the calling of the prophet Samuel and the transition from judges to kings, from theocracy to monarchy. God called Samuel as a young child and set him apart. He anointed Samuel to be a priest and a prophet, and he functioned as the last judge and leader of Israel before the beginning of the monarchy.

Samuel led Israel, calling them to forsake their foreign gods and serve only the Lord. When he became old, he appointed his sons as judges in his place, but they did not walk in the ways of God. The elders of Israel demanded a king instead, just as the nations around them had. They did indeed need a righteous King to lead them, but they had a King they continued to reject. So God told Samuel to give them what they asked for but to warn them of the consequences of an earthly king.

God led Samuel to anoint Saul to be the first king of Israel. He was a rather reluctant king initially, and he soon became prideful and impetuous. Because Saul failed to fully obey the Lord, God rejected Saul as king and removed his spirit from him. God called Samuel to anoint another to be king after Saul's death. God called David the shepherd boy to be the next king of Israel. He was the youngest son of his father Jesse, not even considered a contender for the title. But God "sees not as man sees: man looks on the outward appearance, but the LORD looks on the heart" (1 Sam. 16:7).

So David was called and anointed to be the next king; however, Saul was still alive and on the throne. Saul became jealous of David and tried to kill him many times, but David who had the opportunity to kill Saul, refused to because he would not touch the Lord's anointed. Until Saul died, David would not take his place on the throne. Many years went by with David on the run from Saul, until finally Saul was killed in battle.

David returned and was anointed king over Israel. He led the nation in military battles, extending and securing the boundaries of Israel. He was a great military leader, and the people followed him. Then David fell into sin, committing adultery and murder. When the prophet Nathan came to him and confronted him with his sin, David repented. Because David also composed many of the Psalms, we can read in Psalm 51 his prayer of confession and repentance.

Described as a man after God's own heart, David may lead us to wonder how he could fall so far. That is the beauty of grace. Remember the Bible is not always prescriptive; sometimes it's descriptive.

So, when we see a story in the Bible, such as this narrative of David committing adultery and murder, that's not prescribing how we are to behave just because it says that David was a man after God's own heart. It's describing his actual behavior, because these are real people who lived at a real time in history who were real sinners just like you and me. We see the truth of what actually happened in David's life, but the reason he's a man after God's own heart is that he never turned away from God to worship false gods. He never rejected God; rather, he repented of his sin and turned to God.

That confession and repentance did not wipe away the consequences, however. The son born to David and Bathsheba died. David had more children, but he did not make the best choices as a parent after that. He faced a lot of very sad consequences as a result, including a daughter who was raped, a son who was murdered, and another son who attempted to overthrow him and was eventually killed. David was a man who failed in many ways, but he was a great king with a heart for God.

David desired to build a magnificent temple for God to replace the Tabernacle, which had been designed for travel in the wilderness. Since the capital of Israel had been moved to Jerusalem, the City of David, he wanted to build a permanent place for God's glory to reside. But God desired to make David's name great and establish a house or dynasty through him instead (2 Samuel 7:11). God declared to David through the prophet Nathan that one of his own sons would be the one to build the temple. So, God made a covenant with David that He would establish his throne and his kingdom forever. Known as the Davidic covenant, this promise pointed toward the future hope and restoration that was to come through the line of David—the Messiah, Jesus Christ.

First and Second Samuel are important for showing us the consequences of sin, the need for a Savior, and setting the foundation for the better King who was coming—the Son of David who would bring deliverance, redemption, and who would reign forever.

• •

"'I will raise up your offspring after you, who shall come from your body, and I will establish his kingdom. And your house and your kingdom shall be made sure forever before me. Your throne shall be established forever.'"

2 SAMUEL 7:12b-13

• •

1 AND 2 KINGS

Key Term: Compromise

Key People: Solomon, Elijah, Elisha, Hezekiah, Josiah

The historical narrative of 1 and 2 Kings spans the history of Israel from the death of King David to the fall of Jerusalem. These books were originally one scroll, compiled by an anonymous author from many sources, such as court documents, official records, annals of kings, and possibly records of the prophet Isaiah. The books cover four hundred years of history and could have been the work of two separate compilations, one before and one after the fall of Jerusalem.

Historically, these accounts document the reign of Solomon following the death of David and the division of the kingdom of Israel under Solomon's son Rehoboam. The kingdom split as his rival, Jeroboam, set up a counterfeit reign and religion in Samaria, the capital of what came to be known as the Northern Kingdom of Israel, while Rehoboam ruled over the Southern Kingdom of Judah in Jerusalem. Politically, these books detail the succession of kings that followed. Spiritually, they describe the moral decline of both kingdoms, explaining why Israel and Judah both fell to foreign empires.

First and Second Kings follow First and Second Samuel chronologically, continuing the historical narrative of a nation in covenant with God. As God had promised in Deuteronomy 28, Israel would enjoy His favor and blessings as long as they kept the covenant with the God who delivered them from foreign oppression in Egypt and brought them into a land flowing with milk and honey. But if they failed to keep the covenant and turned to worship idols, forgetting the God who saved them, they would be cursed and undergo the judgment of God. First and Second Kings demonstrate the work of the God who keeps His promises. As the nation fell into moral decline and apostasy, God allowed destruction to come.

After Solomon's death, his son Rehoboam refused to relieve the tax burden on the people, prompting them to rebel against him. The ten northern tribes of Israel made Jeroboam their king, while Solomon's son Rehoboam reigned in Jerusalem over the Southern Kingdom of Judah. In 722 BC, the Northern Kingdom of Israel, which had only a succession of evil kings, was conquered by the Assyrians and exiled. The Southern Kingdom of Judah, the Davidic line, enjoyed some godly kings, such as Hezekiah and Josiah, who revived the worship of God. Because of their national apostasy, however, Judah also fell to foreign powers, being conquered by the Babylonians in 586 BC and exiled to Babylon.

Written from Babylon to a nation in exile, this historical narrative is also theological. The author emphasizes the spiritual and moral reasons for Israel's decline and deportation, yet continues to offer hope to the Jewish exiles. First and Second Kings tell the story of "the relationship of a sovereign God to a responsible people, Israel."[5] The promise of blessings for obedience and curses for disobedience had been clearly articulated through Moses (Deut. 28), but Israel had ignored the warning, as well as the prophets (2 Kings 17:23). The ministries and miracles of Elijah and Elisha, who prophesied God's judgment, are found in 1 and 2 Kings as well. The covenant broken, the sovereign God responded with faithfulness to His word, essentially orchestrating the events that led to Israel's captivity.

The narrative account of 2 Kings teaches theological themes that are continued throughout Scripture: the sovereignty of God over all nations, the covenantal relationship between God and Israel, and the preservation of a remnant through which the Messiah would come and bring redemption to all people. God's sovereignty is seen as He orchestrated events and used the nations surrounding Israel as instruments of judgment. He works in and through people, even those who do not acknowledge Him, to accomplish His will, demonstrating His rule and reign over all creation. These passages written to a nation in exile would have served as both a reminder of God's authority and also a warning to return to the God who reigns over them with both loving-kindness and justice. These Scriptures reveal the same sovereign God to us today. He is still a faithful God who keeps His promises.

God's promise to David of a remnant who would remain in Judah was kept as Jesus came through that line, bringing redemption and hope. Even though Judah had some godly kings, such as Hezekiah, the narrative reveals his failures as well, pointing the reader to the reality of flawed humanity. As Victor Hamilton notes, "The sequencing of these chapters reminds us also that the best of human leaders are flawed and fallible, and Hezekiah, although reformist and godly, is not Messiah. There is really only one leader in whom we may put our trust, and that is in one greater not only than Solomon, but in one greater also than Hezekiah."[6]

Believers today should be encouraged by these passages because they stand as a reminder of God's sovereignty, faithfulness, justice, loving-kindness, redemption, and hope. These words teach the character of God who does not change (Heb. 13:8). They show the nature of humanity and the

---

[5] Kenneth L. Barker and John R. Kohlenberger, *1, 2 Kings, Expositor's Bible Commentary, Abridged Edition: Old Testament* (Grand Rapids: Zondervan, 2017), 488.

[6] Victor P. Hamilton, *Handbook on the Historical Books* (Grand Rapids: Baker Publishing Group, 2001), 461.

problem of sin. They reveal a God who "hears and answers prayer and faithfully keeps His promises."[7] And they point toward the hope that is in the Son of David, who came to fulfill the Law that faithless man could not keep and institute a new covenant based on the faithfulness of God that cannot fail.

* *

"Blessed be the LORD who has
given rest to his people Israel, according
to all that he promised. Not one word
has failed of all his good promise, which
he spoke by Moses his servant."

1 KINGS 8:56

* *

---

[7] Barker and Kohlenberger, *Expositor's Commentary,* 488.

1 AND 2 CHRONICLES

Key Term: Continuity
Key People: David, Solomon, the kings of Israel and Judah

From 1 and 2 Samuel through 1 and 2 Kings, the historical narrative has been mostly chronological. First and Second Samuel narrate the birth and calling of Samuel, then the period of the United Kingdom under Saul and David. First Kings picks up with the death of David and the reign of Solomon, then the division of the kingdom after Solomon's death. Second Kings continues with the succession of kings in both kingdoms and ends with the last king of Judah being released from prison by Babylon, offering hope that there is still a future for Judah and the line of David.

Rather than picking up at the end of 2 Kings and continuing the narrative, 1 and 2 Chronicles were written from a different perspective. First and Second Kings were written to a nation in exile; First and Second Chronicles were written after the Jews returned from exile. First and Second Kings were written from the perspective of the prophets; First and Second Chronicles were written from the perspective of the priests. The Chronicler's purpose was to recount the history of Israel from the beginning, so he starts with Adam and Eve, tracing the genealogy of Israel and her history. Kings and Chronicles complement one another as they describe the same period of history but from two different perspectives, much like the Gospels give us four different perspectives of the life of Christ.

First Chronicles begins with a genealogical account from Adam to Saul and then recounts the story of King David, most likely using 1 and 2 Samuel as sources. The Chronicler focuses on David and the covenant, omitting the story of his affair with Bathsheba, instead pointing to the hope of the Messiah through the Davidic line. He describes the duties of the priesthood as well as the plans for Solomon's temple.

Second Chronicles describes the kings who came after David, beginning with Solomon and the construction of the temple. The Chronicler omits the kings of Israel, focusing instead on the Davidic line that continued in Judah. He emphasized the continuity of David's descendants in Judah, as well as the continuity of worship in Jerusalem. As in 2 Kings, each monarch is described as good or bad, emphasizing the need for a Righteous King to rule God's people. Because Judah tended to have more good kings than evil kings, they lasted longer than Israel did.

The Chronicler recounts the revivals under Hezekiah and Josiah, who led the nation to repent and return to God, renewing the covenant with Him. But because the nation continued to be plagued by unbelief and rebellion, they were conquered by the Babylonians, Jerusalem was destroyed, and the people were exiled to Babylon. Second Chronicles ends on a hopeful note, however. In 539 BC, the Babylonians were defeated by the Persians, and the Persian king, Cyrus, issued a decree that the exiled people could return to Jerusalem and rebuild. Hope remains, as the Chronicler points us toward the future King who reigns with justice and righteousness.

• •

"Therefore David blessed the Lord in the presence of all the assembly. And David said: 'Blessed are you, O Lord, the God of Israel our father, forever and ever. Yours, O Lord, is the greatness and the power and the glory and the victory and the majesty, for all that is in the heavens and in the earth is yours. Yours is the kingdom, O Lord, and you are exalted as head above all.'"

1 CHRONICLES 29:10-11

• •

EZRA

Key Term: Return
Key People: Ezra

In the earliest Hebrew manuscripts, Ezra and Nehemiah were one book. Most scholars believe that the author of 1 and 2 Chronicles also wrote Ezra and Nehemiah because of many similarities in language and style. Jewish tradition ascribes the authorship to Ezra, but we have no evidence to confirm it. The Chronicler, as he is often called, wrote for the restored community after the return to Jerusalem.

After the Jews' captivity and exile to Babylon, God's people lost all hope in the promises of God. Then King Cyrus declared those who wanted to return to Jerusalem could go back and rebuild. After seventy years in Babylon, many of the Jews had been born in captivity. Life in Babylon was all they knew. But some of them were ready to return and reclaim the land God had promised to Abraham.

One hundred and fifty years earlier, Isaiah had prophesied that the Jews would be allowed to return under the decree of a man named Cyrus. The prophet Jeremiah had prophesied that Judah would be exiled for seventy years. Both of these prophecies were fulfilled when Cyrus issued the decree that the Jews could return to Jerusalem.

The Chronicler lists the inventory of articles belonging to the temple which Nebuchadnezzar had carried away when Babylon destroyed Jerusalem. Cyrus returned those items to the Jews. A list of exiles who returned was given, along with the offerings they gave.

They rebuilt the altar and the temple under the leadership of Zerubbabel, which wasn't as grand as the magnificent temple under King Solomon, but they were able to restore their sacrificial system of worship. That was the first step in returning to temple worship, which was their national identity as a people. They faced much opposition because other people were living there by the time of their return, but over time they were able to rebuild and restore their sacrificial system of worship, including the celebration of the feasts.

Ezra was a scribe commissioned by the Persian king to administer God's law in Judah. He came to Jerusalem after the temple was restored and as a scribe skilled in the Law of Moses, Ezra devoted himself to teaching the people the Word of God, its laws and decrees. As both a priest and a scribe, he encouraged the returning exiles to keep the covenant and walk in obedience to God's law. Worship was restored, disobedience to the Mosaic Law was confronted, and the hand of God was seen as God moved on the hearts of those whose decisions made the way for the restoration of God's people to the Promised Land.

Ezra teaches us the importance of the land and the sacrificial system to the nation of Israel. As God's plan of redemption unfolds, we see His faithfulness to His promises and His goodness toward His people despite their rebellion and apostasy. It's a book of great hope in the God who restores those who put their trust in Him.

"'Whoever is among you of all his people, may his God be with him, and let him go up to Jerusalem, which is in Judah, and rebuild the house of the Lord, the God of Israel— he is the God who is in Jerusalem.'"

EZRA 1:3

NEHEMIAH

Key Term: Rebuild
Key People: Nehemiah

Nehemiah arrived in Jerusalem about thirteen years after Ezra. He was a cupbearer to the Persian king and was distressed by a report that Jerusalem was still in shambles with the walls broken down. The temple had been restored, but the walls around Jerusalem were still broken down, destroyed by fire. Walls were important for the defense of a people, and the broken walls represented shame for the returned exiles. He knew the importance of reestablishing Jerusalem and the worship of God's people by rebuilding the walls. The Persian king, Artaxerxes, permitted him to return and provided materials for the walls to be rebuilt.

In these thirteen chapters, Nehemiah prayed, wept, fasted, and acted on what God put in his heart to do. He employed great principles of leadership as he directed men by families to rebuild different sections of the wall, finishing the work in just fifty-two days. They, too, worked amid opposition by their enemies, but God's hand was upon the work, and He blessed them with favor. As they prayed and worked, God guarded and protected them.

Nehemiah includes more lists, including a list of the returned exiles and all the gifts that were given for the temple. When the walls were finished, they held a great assembly, reading and teaching the Word of God, confessing and repenting of sin, and reviving their devotion to God. They renewed their covenant with God, sealing it with the names of their leaders, Levites, and priests. The wall was dedicated, the work of the Levites restored, and offerings to the Lord reestablished.

The books of Ezra and Nehemiah demonstrate that God is faithful to forgive and restore those who turn to Him in repentance. He works for the good of His people to accomplish His will and to fulfill His Word. God was true to His covenant with Abraham to bless his descendants with the Promised Land and the future hope to be a blessing to all other nations. And He was true to His covenant to David to bless him with an eternal kingdom, as his heirs would maintain the throne. The remnant who returned to Jerusalem and Judah included the men who reestablished Bethlehem where, five hundred years later, the Son of David would be born, bringing eternal hope to all the world.

"And Ezra opened the book in the sight of all the people, for he was above all the people, and as he opened it all the people stood. And Ezra blessed the Lord, the great God, and all the people answered, 'Amen, Amen,' lifting up their hands. And they bowed their heads and worshiped the Lord with their faces to the ground."

NEHEMIAH 8:5-6

ESTHER

Key Term: Chosen
Key People: Esther, Mordecai, King Xerxes, Haman

Esther is the historical narrative of those Jews who remained in the Persian Empire and either did not return or had not yet returned to Jerusalem. Esther was a Jewish girl who became a Persian queen, placing her in the right place at the right time to be the instrument God used to maintain the Jewish race. She found out about a plot by an evil man, Haman, to extinguish all the Jewish people. Esther risked her life to go to the king without being summoned and to plead on behalf of her people. If Haman had succeeded in his plan, the Jews would have been exterminated and God's promises to Abraham and David would have failed. But because of Esther's courage and trust in God, He intervened and stopped Haman, sparing the Jews from extinction.

Esther is the only book of the Bible where God's name is not mentioned, but we see His hand at work so providentially from beginning to end. God's devotion to His people never wavered. He was continually working to redeem them and draw them back to himself. We see that time and time again through the judges, through the prophets, and even through the rule of foreign empires. God not only keeps His promises, but He works providentially to bring them to pass.

The author of Esther also explains to us the origin of the Feast of Purim. It was a Jewish feast not outlined in the Mosaic Law, but one that originated with the celebration of God's deliverance from extinction. The writer of Esther encourages the Jews to continue to celebrate Purim as a remembrance of what God had done. For believers today, this narrative is an encouragement that our sovereign God keeps His promises and watches over His own. He is working in response to our petitions, even when we cannot see it.

"'For if you keep silent at this time, relief and deliverance will rise for the Jews from another place, but you and your father's house will perish. And who knows whether you have not come to the kingdom for such a time as this?'"

ESTHER 4:14

The Wisdom &
Poetic Books
The Writings

THE WISDOM & POETIC
Books

The wisdom and poetic books are read and interpreted differently because they're a different literary genre than historical narrative. Wisdom literature is an ancient literary style that originated in the Near East. While there can be some element of historical narrative within them (such as with Job), this genre consists of sayings or teachings on wisdom, which is the ability to apply God's principles to one's life. The purpose of this genre is to teach, especially the young, how to live out the principles of godliness and wisdom in the world. These books serve as guides for godly living through practical instruction, understanding about the ways of the world, and descriptions of different types of people, such as the wise, the fool, and the simple.

Poetry is a style of writing that typically uses meter, imagery, and figurative language to communicate ideas. Hebrew poetry, in particular, has some unique characteristics, such as parallelism, and it lacks rhyme or meter. Understanding how figurative language works is important in understanding how to interpret poetry.

With these five books, the wisdom and poetic styles overlap somewhat; for instance, Job has characteristics of both wisdom and poetic language. The Psalms are mostly poetic, while Proverbs is mostly wisdom literature. Ecclesiastes is typically wisdom literature, and Song of Solomon is primarily poetic.

JOB

Key Term: Pain

Job is a unique book of the Bible, probably set in the time of the patriarchs—Abraham, Isaac, and Jacob. While we do not know the author of this book, we do know the setting is the land of Uz. Although Job is not an Israelite, he does know Israel's God. This book does not continue any of the historical narrative or seem to fit within the context of the overall story of Israel, but it does give great insight into the nature and character of God.

Job was written in this ancient style to show God is sovereign and He can be trusted even in our suffering. We may never understand why God allows bad things to happen, but we do know from the Garden account that sin has proliferated within our world. Sin brings suffering; and because we have free will, people suffer sometimes at the hands of others. Trials also come simply because we live in a world marred by the Fall. The Creation God intended to be perfect has been corrupted, and the result is a world in which we experience natural disasters, famine, and chaos. But what we can learn from Job is God is in the midst of it with us. The Bible never promises that we will be free of pain. In fact, Jesus said there *would be* trouble in this world.

> *"In the world you will have tribulation. But take heart; I have overcome the world"* (John 16:33).

The hope in Jesus' statement is that He is sovereign over our suffering. And that is a truth Job learned in his trial. Unbeknownst to Job, Satan was the one who caused Job's suffering, not God. But Satan was limited in power by the authority and sovereignty of Almighty God. Job was a righteous man whom God allowed Satan to afflict with pain and loss. Job struggled to understand why he was suffering because many of the ancients believed that suffering was always the result of sin. Job's friends brought him no comfort, only encouraging him to repent so that God would have mercy on him. But Job maintained his innocence before God.

Job desired to make his case before God. He wanted an arbiter, someone who could go before God on his behalf, reminding us that Jesus would one day stand in our place before the Father. Job complained that his friends offered no comfort and his God offered no remedy. Job acknowledged that God created him, that God held all wisdom, that God was all-powerful, and that God was his hope. But his friends accused him of unrepentant sin, of not fearing God, and of too much pride. They wanted Job to admit his unrighteousness; Job wanted God to be just.

When God finally responded to Job, He revealed His majesty, power, knowledge, and justice. Job was humbled by God's presence and His Words, and he repented before God. God rebuked Job's friends who did not speak rightly of Him or bring any comfort to Job in his suffering. And then He commended Job because he *did* speak rightly of God when he acknowledged His goodness. Job knew that his suffering did not reflect the heart of God. What Job did not know is that the suffering was at the hand of Satan. He was actually right that all the pain and agony and loss did not come from the hand of God but reflected the character of the Accuser.

The book of Job teaches us that God is good, sovereign, and just. He's not the author of our pain and suffering, although He does sometimes allow it. We may not understand it, but we can take comfort in His presence, His goodness, and His sovereignty. One day, all things will be restored because God is just. He brings beauty from ashes. We know that even when God allows suffering in our lives, He always has our best at heart because that's who He is. Daniel J. Estes states: "In the final analysis, Job compels us to trust the character of God when we are unable to comprehend his ways."[8] And sometimes we only see His nature clearly when our suffering renders us unable to see anything else.

· ·

"'I had heard of you by the hearing
of the ear, but now my eye sees you."

JOB 42:5

· ·

---

[8] Daniel J. Estes, *Handbook on the Wisdom Books and Psalms* (Grand Rapids: Baker Academic, 2005), 128.

PSALMS

Key Term: Personal

The Psalms are a collection of songs written by different people at different times in Israel's history. About half of them were written by King David, and others are written by Asaph, the sons of Korah, Moses, and Solomon. Probably compiled after the return of the Jews from exile, the Psalter was the songbook for Israel's worship. The 150 psalms are divided into the following Books:

Book 1 | Psalms 1-41 (mostly psalms of David)

Book 2 | Psalms 42-72 (some by David, the sons of Korah, and Solomon)

Book 3 | Psalms 73-89 (psalms of Asaph and the sons of Korah)

Book 4 | Psalms 90-106 (Psalm 90 by Moses, the rest are anonymous)

Book 5 | Psalms 107-150 (more by David, the rest are anonymous)

The Psalms demonstrate the whole range of human experience and emotion, expressed through the poetic use of figurative language. They are "intimate expressions of personal dialogue with God."[9] Some of them recount history, some are cries for justice and pleas for help, some are laments (expressions of grief or sorrow), and some are psalms of praise and thanksgiving.

There are a few basic types of psalms, although some tend to overlap categories. These classifications can help us understand how to interpret the meaning and significance of the text.

Wisdom Psalms | 1, 34, 35, 37, 49, 50, 73, 112

The wisdom psalms, similar to Proverbs, teach the benefits of choosing to live by God's standards of right and wrong as established in the Law. They primarily highlight the differences between righteousness and wickedness, encouraging the reader to live rightly.

---

[9] Ibid., 151.

Royal Psalms | 2, 18, 20, 21, 45, 72, 101, 110, 144

The royal psalms describe the life of the king, godly leadership, and the Davidic covenant. Some of these are Messianic as well, pointing toward the ultimate fulfillment in King Jesus. They remind us of what godly leadership should be and the hope we have in our King.

Individual Laments | 3, 4, 5, 7, 10, 13, 17, 28, 31, 39, 55, 56, 57, 59, 69, 70, 71, 86, 88, 102, 109, 141, 142, 143

Individual laments are psalms of grief due to suffering. The psalmist turns his mourning toward God and seeks His comfort. They are prayers to God that show us how we too can turn to God in times of suffering and grief.

Community Laments | 12, 14, 36, 44, 53, 54, 58, 60, 61, 74, 77, 79, 80, 82, 83, 85, 89, 90, 94, 108, 137, 140

Community laments are corporate gatherings in which the people collectively turn to God in times of distress and suffering. They encourage us as the body of Christ to trust in God for His peace and comfort.

Hymns of Thanksgiving and Praise | 8, 9, 15, 23, 24, 26, 29, 30, 33, 40, 41, 42, 43, 46, 47, 48, 65, 66, 68, 75, 76, 84, 87, 92, 93, 96, 97, 98, 99, 100, 103, 104, 107, 111, 135, 136, 138, 139, 145, 147, 148, 149, 150

These psalms express gratitude to God and praise for His mighty works, His creation, His victory over their enemies, His guidance, His deliverance, His glory, etc. They lead us to praise Him as well.

Confidence Psalms | 11, 16, 27, 52, 62, 63, 64, 67, 91, 146

These are confessions of confidence and trust in God amid times of danger and uncertainty. They remind us to put our confidence in the Lord.

Celebrations of the Law | 19, 119

These two powerful psalms are poetic tributes to the Word of God and its power in the lives of God's people. They serve as reminders to value and honor God's Word in our own lives.

Messianic Psalm | 22

This royal psalm stands alone as a prophetic and Messianic psalm. King David wrote of his despair prophetically speaking of Jesus' crucifixion as well. Jesus quoted this psalm from the cross.

Penitential Psalms | 6, 25, 32, 38, 51, 143

The penitential psalms are cries for forgiveness of sins and restoration of the relationship between the psalmist and God. They express the suffering of the psalmist as a result of his sin and the desire to be reunited to fellowship with God. They are helpful guides for prayer of repentance for us as well.

Historical Psalms | 78, 81, 95, 105, 106

These psalms recount the history of Israel in poetic form as reminders to the people of His faithfulness. They remind us of His faithfulness still.

The Hallel | 113-118

These six psalms were sung during Jewish festivals as part of their temple liturgy. They came to be part of the Passover meal, with Psalms 113 and 114 sung before the meal and Psalms 115-118 sung afterward.[10]

---

[10] Barker, *NIV Study Bible*, 908.

Songs of Ascent | 120-134

These psalms were sung during the annual pilgrimages to Jerusalem for the festivals and possibly were also used as part of the temple liturgy. They focus on God as the source of help, His presence in the sanctuary, His faithfulness to the Israelites, and the One who delivers them from their enemies.[11]

Many of the psalms have introductions that provide the context for the song. This background is especially helpful when studying the psalms of David because we can read his responses to particular events in his life.

David's Psalms with corresponding events:

> Psalm 3: 2 Samuel 15-17
>
> Psalm 18: 2 Samuel 22
>
> Psalm 30: 1 Kings 8:63
>
> Psalm 34: 1 Samuel 21:12-22:1
>
> Psalm 51: 2 Samuel 11-12
>
> Psalm 52: 1 Samuel 22:9-19
>
> Psalm 54: 1 Samuel 23:19
>
> Psalm 56: 1 Samuel 21:10-11
>
> Psalm 57: 1 Samuel 22:1 or 24:3
>
> Psalm 59: 1 Samuel 19:11
>
> Psalm 60: 2 Samuel 8:1-14
>
> Psalm 63: 2 Samuel 8:1-14
>
> Psalm 142: 1 Samuel 22:1 or 24:3

---

[11] Ibid., 922.

We also have several literary devices used in the Psalms. Hebrew poetry is uniquely characterized by parallelism and the use of acrostics such as Psalm 119, which is the longest of those. Hebrew poetry also contains imagery, hyperbole, metaphors, and similes.

FIGURATIVE LANGUAGE IN THE PSALMS

TERM	DEFINITION	EXAMPLE
Parallelism	Lines in poetry in which the second line repeats, contrasts, or completes the first line	"The heavens declare the glory of God, and the sky above proclaims his handiwork" (19:1)
Acrostic	Each successive letter of the Hebrew alphabet is used at the beginning of each stanza	Psalms 25; 34; 37; 111; 112; 119; 145
Imagery	Use of words that invoke the senses, especially visually	"He lays the beams of his chambers on the waters; he makes the clouds his chariot; he rides on the wings of the wind" (104:3).
Hyperbole	A figure of speech that uses extreme exaggeration to make a point	"God looks down from heaven on the children of men to see if there are any who understand, who seek after God. They have all fallen away; together they have become corrupt; there is none who does good, not even one" (53:2-3).
Metaphor	A figure of speech that makes a comparison between two unlike things	"The LORD is my rock and my fortress and my deliverer, my God, my rock, in whom I take refuge, my shield, and the horn of my salvation, my stronghold" (18:2).
Simile	A figure of speech that makes a comparison using *like* or *as*	"He is like a tree planted by streams of water that yields its fruit in season, and its leaf does not wither" (1:3).
Personification	Ascribing human characteristics to inanimate objects	"When the waters saw you, O God, they were afraid; indeed, the deep trembled" (77:16).

The Psalms touch us with personal examples of worship, prayer, praise, confession, thanksgiving, and wisdom that encourage, comfort, and guide us in our devotion to God.

· ·

"Teach me your way, O Lord,
That I may walk in your truth;
Unite my heart to fear your name.
I give thanks to you, O Lord
my God, with my whole heart,
And I will glorify your name forever.
For great is your steadfast love toward me;
You have delivered my soul
from the depths of Sheol."

PSALM 86:11-13

· ·

PROVERBS

Key Term: Practical

Proverbs is strictly a wisdom book. Wisdom literature is characterized by proverbs or brief sayings that make practical points. There are proverbs outside of the Bible in other ancient cultures, such as Far and Near Eastern literature. Proverbs are meant to be easy to remember; that's why they're short, pithy statements. The proverbs in the Bible are all about wisdom: how to walk with wisdom and how to live out our faith in practical ways that honor God. They're meant to give us instruction in the ways of God and discipleship. Compiled mainly by Solomon, these practical statements reflect the values and morals of those who seek God.

The first nine chapters encourage the reader to seek wisdom above all else, and that wisdom is found in the fear of the Lord. The proverbs that follow are principles regarding many areas of everyday life, such as marriage, discipline, friendship, gossip, laziness, hard work, parenting, pride, temper, wealth, and generosity. We learn the ways of the wise and the ways of the foolish, which are starkly contrasted in these sayings.

One application to keep in mind is that proverbs were intended to be expressions of truth but not promises of God. As Fee and Stuart note in their book *How to Read the Bible for All Its Worth*, "Proverbs set forth a wise way to approach certain practical goals, but do so in terms that cannot be treated like a divine guarantee of success. The particular blessings, rewards, and opportunities mentioned in Proverbs are likely to follow if one will choose the wise courses of action outlined in the poetic, figurative language of the book."[12]

For instance, Proverbs 16:2 reads "Commit your work to the LORD, and your plans will be established." This statement is a general principle that we can follow. It's a guideline for wise behavior. However, it is possible to commit our work to the Lord and not see our plans established. Perhaps our plans did not align with God's will. Maybe other factors impacted the results of our work. The verse is not a promise or guarantee from God; it was originally intended, as all proverbs in their ancient context, to be a general principle of wisdom.

The last couple of chapters in Proverbs are poems by Agur and Lemuel. Agur described what life is like when we live by God's wisdom. Lemuel shared an acrostic describing the woman who seeks

---

[12] Gordan D. Fee and Douglas Stuart, *How to Read the Bible for All Its Worth,* 4th. Ed. (Grand Rapids: Zondervan, 2014), 243.

God's wisdom in her life. She is an ideal example of what it means to fear the Lord and live by His principles. She is a woman of excellence, a faithful wife, a hard worker, a generous manager, and a loving mother. She is kind, generous, thoughtful, strong, dignified, wise, and worthy of praise. These characteristics describe not a perfect person but an ideal example to emulate.

The book of Proverbs provides us with practical guidelines for living out the principles of wisdom that reflect the fear of God, and that wisdom points us toward Christ "in whom are hidden all the treasures of wisdom and knowledge" (Col. 2:3).

· ·

"The fear of the LORD is the beginning of knowledge, but fools despise wisdom and discipline."

PROVERBS 1:7

· ·

ECCLESIASTES

Key Term: Purpose

Another example of ancient wisdom literature, Ecclesiastes is sometimes difficult to read and understand. Most likely written by Solomon, it explores the meaning and purpose of life in a fallen and broken world. The writer explores some of the most philosophical and existential questions we all consider at some point in our lives.

Not only was Solomon gifted by God with wisdom, but he was also blessed with riches, honor, and pleasures. When he considered all those qualities, he realized that none of them could truly satisfy or give meaning to life. The writer says everything in life is vanity or meaningless. The Hebrew used here is *hebel*, meaning "vapor," "breath," or "emptiness."[13] And while his tone throughout most of the book seems pessimistic and hopeless, the book has to be read in its entirety to understand its full purpose. The writer's conclusion reveals the wisdom in serving God.

Solomon described the meaninglessness of wisdom because with more knowledge came more grief. He described the vanity of pleasure and hard work. When he surveyed all he had done, it meant nothing. A man may labor both day and night and have nothing to show for it but pain, grief, and a restless mind. He says there is a time for everything, including sorrow, war, and death. None of the blessings in life could make up for all the suffering, so what is the purpose of it all?

Then Solomon concludes his wisdom writing with these words:

> *"The end of the matter; all has been heard. Fear God and keep his commandments, for this is the whole duty of man. For God will bring every deed into judgment, with every secret thing, whether good or evil" (12:13).*

In other words, life apart from God truly is meaningless. Solomon's wrestling with the questions of purpose and significance is summed up in this truth, pointing us toward a God-centered worldview.[14] Solomon demonstrated that a life centered on the self is meaningless—accumulating possessions, seeking honor or fame, and desiring to accomplish great things. All these end in the same meaningless

---

[13] Estes, *Handbook,* 281.

[14] Ibid., 280.

state. Our life is but a breath—here today and gone tomorrow. The only thing that matters is a life lived for God. That is the conclusion of the whole matter.

This philosophical reasoning of Solomon drives us to the hope of the Gospel. Jesus said, "I am the vine; you are the branches. Whoever abides in me and I in him, he it is that bears much fruit, for apart from me you can do nothing" (John 15:5).

SONG OF SOLOMON OR SONG OF SONGS

Key Term: Passion

The Song of Solomon is a beautiful poetic celebration of the beauty of love and marriage. Traditionally ascribed to Solomon, the writing is in the style of "lyric wisdom."[15] The poem consists of a dialogue between a bride and her groom as they anticipate the culmination of their romance through marriage. Some of the figurative language may seem ancient and obscure to us, such as comparing the bride to a horse or her teeth to a flock of sheep. But what does shine through is the love, passion, and devotion they have for one another.

The early Jewish tradition was to approach the Song of Solomon as an allegory of the love of God for Israel.[16] They interpreted the song as a description of the covenant relationship between them and Yahweh. The early church may also have read the Song of Solomon in that way, as both about marriage and about the love between Christ and the church.[17] Ephesians 5:22-33 supports this view as Paul describes marriage as a reflection of the relationship of Jesus to the church. More modern commentators view the song as simply a poetic description of the beauty of married love. Regardless, the Song of Solomon teaches us about purity, the covenantal relationship of marriage, and the power of love.

The Song of Solomon teaches that "monogamous, heterosexual marriage was the proper context for sexual activity according to God's revelation in the Old Testament, and God-fearing Israelites would regard the book in that light."[18] When interpreted this way, sex is seen as a gift from God to be delighted in and cherished. The song recognizes the loyalty, selflessness, and purity of married love.

According to Henrietta Mears in her book *What the Bible Is All About*, the Jewish people likened Proverbs to the outer court of the Tabernacle because it was practical wisdom for walking through daily life.[19] The outer court contained the laver, where the priests washed before making sacrifices, and the altar of sacrifice. If we come to God with clean hands and a surrendered heart, we will be able

---

[15] Fee and Stuart, *How to Read the Bible,* 254.

[16] Estes, *Handbook,* 397.

[17] Ibid.

[18] Fee and Stuart, *How to Read the Bible,* 256.

[19] Henrietta Mears, *What the Bible Is All About,* 2nd rev. ed. (Ventura, CA: Regal Books, 1997), 208.

to receive instruction from the Proverbs and apply those principles of wisdom to our daily lives.[20] They likened Ecclesiastes to the holy place because it draws the reader into the meaning of life and more personal things. The Song of Solomon was likened to the most holy place because that's where the presence of God dwelled. So the Jewish people viewed the Song of Solomon very much as a poetic description of the intimacy between God and His people.

"""Many waters cannot quench love, neither can floods drown it."'

SONG OF SOLOMON 8:7a

---

[20] Ibid.

The Prophetic Books

The Call

THE PROPHETIC
Books

The prophetic books of the Old Testament are probably the least read and least understood of all the books of Scripture. Because they were written to particular people at a particular time in world history, we often struggle to comprehend their significance in our own lives. Understanding the chronological, historical, and cultural context of these books is the key to grasping their relevance.

Of the seventeen prophetic books, four are considered the Major Prophets (Isaiah, Jeremiah, Ezekiel, and Daniel) with the remaining designated as the Minor Prophets. These labels are misleading, however, because they only refer to the length of the original documents, not their importance. Because they are ordered roughly by length in our English Bible, the chronology can be confusing. A more helpful approach is to study these books in light of their place in history.

Covering the period from approximately 780 to 460 BC, the prophetic books can be placed somewhat chronologically according to the history of Israel. Because the dating cannot be exactly determined for all of the books, there may be some overlap in how scholars order them chronologically, but the approximate timing and audience are the keys to understanding their messages. The prophets were men called by God to communicate His Word to His people. Their roles included reminding the Jews of their covenant relationship with Yahweh and warning them of the consequences of failing to keep the Law. The consequences included the destruction of both the Northern and Southern Kingdoms and their captivity and exile to foreign lands. But the prophets also spoke words of hope and redemption in their future, calling to mind the words of Deuteronomy 4:24-31:

> When you father children and children's children, and have grown old in the land, if you act corruptly by making a carved image in the form of anything, and by doing what is evil in the sight of the LORD your God, so as to provoke him to anger, I call heaven and earth to witness against you today, that you will utterly perish from the land that you are going over the Jordan to possess. You will not live long in it, but will be utterly destroyed. And the LORD will scatter you among the peoples, and you will be left few in number among the nations where the LORD will drive you. And there you will serve gods of wood and stone, the work of human hands, that

neither see, nor hear, nor eat, nor smell. But from there you will seek the LORD your God and you will find him, if you search after him with all your heart and with all your soul. When you are in tribulation, and all these things come upon you in the latter days, you will return to the LORD your God and obey his voice. For the LORD your God is a merciful God. He will not leave you or forget the covenant with your fathers that he swore to them.

The prophetic books are written in a combination of prose, poetry, oracles, and symbolic language that can sometimes make them difficult to understand. Just as the historical narratives contained some prophecy, the prophetic books contain some historical narrative. In the narratives, we saw prophets such as Samuel, Nathan, Huldah, Elijah, and Elisha. Their words and actions were described as part of the narratives. Here in the prophetic books, we read their words of warning, encouragement, judgment, and hope, as these men communicated God's Word—once given through the Law, now shared through the prophets as they responded to the divine calling of God.

The nature of prophecy itself is sometimes difficult to read and follow. Not all prophecy was for Israel; some of the prophets spoke to other nations, such as Edom and Assyria. Not all prophetic writings included predictions of future events. The prophets were God's mouthpiece, communicating His truth to the people. Some prophecies did contain predictions, however. It is helpful to understand that some prophecies had an immediate context, an ongoing context, and an ultimate fulfillment. Many of the future prophetic events of the Old Testament have already been fulfilled. These Scriptures are reminders to us of the faithfulness and sovereignty of God.

Those prophecies of the Messiah that have yet to be fulfilled are an encouragement to believers today. Not one word of what God has spoken will fail to come to pass. He was faithful then. He is faithful now.

TIMELINE OF THE PROPHETS

PERIOD OF HISTORY	PROPHET	RECIPIENT	MESSAGE
Pre-exile Mid 800s-585 BC	Joel	Judah	Warned to repent
	Jonah	Assyria	Warned to repent
	Amos	Israel	Warned to repent
	Hosea	Israel	God still loved them
	Isaiah	Judah	The Hope of the Messiah
	Micah	Judah	Judgment/mercy
	Israel conquered and exiled in 722 BC		
	Nahum	Judah	Assyria will fall
	Zephaniah	Judah	Warning to repent/hope of Messiah
	Jeremiah	Judah	Judgment but hope
	Habakkuk	Judah	Live by faith
	Judah conquered and exiled in 586 BC		
Babylonian Exile 586-530 BC	Obadiah	Edom	Judgment was coming
	Daniel	Exiles in Babylon/Persia	Be faithful, future prophecies of Messiah
	Ezekiel	Exiles in Babylon	Visions, God's presence removed from Jerusalem
	Exiles return 535-529 BC		
Post-exile 530-420 BC	Haggai	Judah	Rebuild
	Zechariah	Judah	Visions, Messiah will come
	Malachi	Judah	God's steadfast love

THE PRE-EXILE Prophets

JOEL (835-800 BC)

Key Term: Warned
Recipient: Judah, Pre-exile

Joel was a priest and prophet who called Judah to return to God following a plague of locusts that had destroyed their crops. Not much information exists about Joel or the context of his writing, and some scholars date the book much later. Regardless, Joel's message is simple: He called upon Israel to repent and return to the Lord.

The prophet's warning brings to mind the promises of Deuteronomy 28—blessings for obedience and curses for disobedience. "The presence of grain, wine, and oil is evidence of God's covenant blessings, and their absence is evidence of his judgment."[21] True to His word, God's purpose in allowing devastation is to draw their hearts back to Him.

Joel prophesied a Day of the Lord in which God would pour out His Spirit on all people, bringing both judgment and restoration. God longed to restore what the locusts had eaten and bless His people if only they would return to Him in repentance and commitment to the covenant.

Joel teaches us about the character of God. He is faithful to His covenant promises to Israel; He is both just and merciful; and He is righteous and gracious.

---

[21] W. Brian Aucker, "Joel," in *The ESV Women's Study Bible,* gen. ed. Wayne Grudem (Wheaton, IL: Crossway, 2020), 1361.

"'Yet even now,' declares the LORD,
'return to me with all your heart, with fasting,
with weeping, and with mourning.'"

JOEL 2:12

JONAH (790 BC)

Key Term: Reluctant
Recipient: Assyria

Unlike other prophetic books, Jonah is a historical narrative with a prophetic message. Jonah was a reluctant prophet during a time of peace and prosperity for Israel's Northern Kingdom. Israel had experienced victory over Damascus, resulting in pride and the expectation that God would bring judgment on all of their enemies. But God called Jonah to announce the coming judgment to Assyria so that they might repent.

He ran from God's call to preach to the people of Ninevah, the capital of Assyria, who were known to be cruel and evil people and a threat to Israel. God wanted Jonah to warn them of destruction if they did not repent of their wickedness. Jonah knew if they repented, God would extend forgiveness to the enemy.

Jonah boarded a ship to escape God's calling, but God didn't let him off the hook. After a storm threatened the lives of everyone on the ship, Jonah was thrown overboard where he was swallowed by a fish. After the fish spit him out, he returned to Ninevah and called the people to repentance. They responded to the Word of God and repented of their sins. God showed compassion and relented from bringing disaster on them, which angered Jonah. Jonah wanted God to only show compassion to Israel, but God shows His compassion and mercy for all those who will repent.

Jonah teaches that God's love and compassion extend to all people who will repent and put their trust in Him. It encourages us to be faithful to God's calling and trust Him with the results.

. . . .

"'I called out to the LORD out of my distress, and he answered me."

JONAH 2:2a

. . . .

AMOS (767-743 BC)

Key Term: Immoral
Recipient: Israel, Pre-exile

Amos was a shepherd and farmer whom God called to be a prophet. Israel, under the reign of Jeroboam, was prosperous and wealthy. But in their pride, they ignored the laws about justice and morality. They oppressed the poor and worshiped idols. They ignored God's commands and were unfaithful to His covenant. During this peaceful and prosperous time, the Israelites grew prideful and expected God to keep His covenant to protect and prosper them, but they failed to keep their commitment to follow the law. "It was also a time of idolatry, extravagant indulgences in luxurious living, immorality, corruption of judicial procedures, and oppression of the poor."[22] The Israelites had grown complacent and smug in their special status as God's people, forgetting they were subject to His judgments like the other nations.

Amos warned the Israelites of impending judgment for their immorality and their failure to keep His covenant. He called the Israelites to righteousness and justice for the oppressed. He reminded them that He is sovereign over all the nations, not just Israel.

He also promised a time of restoration that would come through the House of David, a promise fulfilled in Jesus, the Son of David, seven hundred years later. Even in judgment for their sin, there is hope for those who repent and turn back to God.

Amos teaches us that God is righteous and just. He cares about how we live and how we treat others. He calls us to be people who walk in righteousness and work for justice for the oppressed.

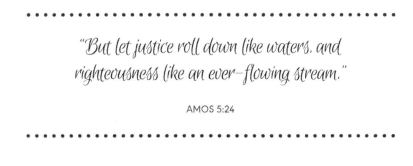

"But let justice roll down like waters, and righteousness like an ever-flowing stream."

AMOS 5:24

---

[22] Barker, *NIV Study Bible,* 1345.

HOSEA (755-725 BC)

Key Term: Unfaithful
Recipient: Israel, Pre-exile

Hosea lived in the final days leading up to Israel's fall to the Assyrian Empire. The kings of the Northern Kingdom of Israel had rebelled against God and His law repeatedly, leading the people further into sin. Like an unfaithful wife, Israel had forsaken the Lord for other pursuits. God called Hosea to live out the prophecy to Israel as a sort of dramatic visual to the people, who were unfaithful to the covenant with God. Hosea was instructed to marry Gomer, an unfaithful and adulterous woman, as a symbol of Israel's infidelity toward God. Yet when Gomer abandoned her marriage, God instructed Hosea to redeem her and be faithful to her despite her sin as an example of His redeeming love for Israel.

The book of Hosea teaches us about God's faithful love. He is patient and steadfast, calling sinners to repent and return to Him, and offering grace and forgiveness to those who do. Israel was still called to repent or face judgment. Just as a loving parent must discipline a wayward child, God lovingly called His people to return so that He might show them mercy. Because of their rebellious ways, Israel eventually fell to the Assyrians, God's tool of judgment for their rebellion and apostasy.

Hosea teaches us that God does call us to faithfulness. We are under a new covenant in Christ, but God still wants our hearts. He is worthy of our faithful love and obedience. Yet, even when we fail Him, He is patient and longsuffering, calling us back to His redeeming love.

. . . .

"Sow for yourselves righteousness; reap steadfast love; break up your fallow ground, for it is the time to seek the LORD, that he may come and rain righteousness upon you."

HOSEA 10:12

. . . .

ISAIAH (739-631 BC)

Key Term: Promised
Recipient: Judah, Pre-exile

Using both prose and poetry, Isaiah wrote to the nation of Judah, calling them back to faithfulness and devotion to God and His covenant. The prophet Isaiah spoke of the reasons for the coming judgment: Israel and Judah had become corrupt, their leaders having rejected God and His commands and sought alliances with other nations, rather than depending on God to defend them. Isaiah prophesied the coming judgment at the hands of Assyria against the Northern Kingdom and Babylon against the Southern Kingdom. Even though God would use Assyria and Babylon as His tools of punishment on Israel and Judah, He promised that those other nations would also be held accountable for their sin.

But Isaiah's prophecy doesn't end with only promises of judgment. Isaiah promised restoration as well. Isaiah prophesied of a remnant who would survive and return to the land in fulfillment of God's covenant with Abraham. And he spoke of a Servant who would come to bring healing and restoration from the line of David, in keeping with the Davidic covenant. The suffering Servant would suffer and die for the sins of the people, but this Messiah would also reign over sin and make all things new.

Isaiah contains many prophecies of Jesus, especially Isaiah 9:6-7; 11; 52-53; and 61, which Jesus quoted about Himself in Luke 4:16-21. Israel's hope lay in these promises of a Messiah who would deliver them from the bondage of sin and bring salvation. Isaiah used some of the most tender and loving examples and language in all the prophetic books, reminding us that even amid God's just judgment, His love for His people never wavers.

. . . .

"For unto us a child is born, to us a son is given; and the government shall be upon his shoulder, and he shall be called Wonderful Counselor, Mighty God, Everlasting Father, Prince of Peace."

ISAIAH 9:6

. . . .

MICAH (740-700 BC)

Key Term: Judged
Recipient: Judah, Pre-exile

Micah prophesied to Judah during the same time as Amos, Hosea, and Isaiah. He called on the people to repent and turn from their sins of idolatry, greed, and immorality. If they would not turn back to God, they would face His judgment because God is just and faithful to His covenant promises. Micah used the language of a courtroom and declared God's case against Judah and its capital, Jerusalem. Their sin demanded judgment, and though God longed to be gracious, He could not fail to be just.

Micah described a vision in which he saw God's glory depart from the temple in Jerusalem. This was a significant indictment against Judah because God has always desired to dwell among His people. The tabernacle and later the temple were designed so that a holy God could live among a sinful people. But they had failed to keep the requirements for sacrificial worship. They worshiped other gods, lacked godly leadership, offered sacrifices without repentance, and denied to show integrity in business. Because they failed to keep the covenant requirements of justice, mercy, and faithfulness, God's presence would depart from among them.

But even though His glory would leave from the temple, He promised to one day send a King to bring His presence back into their midst, the coming Messiah who would bring deliverance and redemption. Like the other prophets, Micah promised their punishment would not last forever because God still desires to dwell with His people.

Micah reminds us that God should be the object of our worship from the heart. Out of His steadfast love and faithfulness, He remains true to His promise of mercy and forgiveness for those who turn to Him in repentance and trust.

• •

*"He has told you, O man, what is good;
and what does the LORD require of you
but to do justice, and to love kindness,
and to walk humbly with your God?"*

MICAH 6:8

• •

NAHUM (640-612 BC)

Key Term: Proud
Recipient: Judah (about Assyria)

Nahum's prophecy comes after the Northern Kingdom's fall at the hands of the Assyrian Empire in 722 BC. The Bible makes clear that Israel's destruction and exile were a result of their rebellion and idolatry. They had been warned repeatedly, yet failed to return to God. The result was exactly as God had promised: they were conquered by Assyria and removed from the Promised Land, while Assyria repopulated the land with foreigners. It was a dark time in Israel's history.

Yet God called Nahum to speak words of hope and comfort to Judah: Justice would come to Assyria as well. The Assyrian Empire was known to be ruthless and bloodthirsty. They were evil, brutal people who committed atrocities against God's people. It's the reason Jonah ran from God's call to preach to them 150 years earlier. He wanted retribution for them, not repentance. And Nineveh, the Assyrian capital, did experience a short time of repentance. But it didn't last, and God used Nahum to pronounce judgment on Assyria for their pride and wickedness. They, too, would eventually fall.

This word was a comfort to God's people because they were assured of His perfect justice. He is a refuge for those who put their trust in Him. And He will not tolerate evil forever. Nahum reminds us that we can trust His justice for all the evil we see in the world today. While we still experience suffering in this fallen world, we do so with the assurance that God's justice will one day right every wrong, and God's people will experience His eternal comfort.

- -

*"The LORD is good, a stronghold
in the day of trouble; he knows
those who take refuge in him."*

NAHUM 1:7

- -

ZEPHANIAH (630 BC)

Key Term: Urged
Recipient: Judah, Pre-exile

Zephaniah prophesied during the reign of Josiah to announce the coming judgment of Judah and her capital, Jerusalem. Josiah was an exceptional king who honored God's Word, tore down the altars to idols, restored worship, and led Judah to renew the covenant with God. Nevertheless, their revival was short-lived. Evil kings before and after Josiah still influenced Judah, and they still faced the consequences of their idolatry and rebellion.

Zephaniah also prophesied the destruction of surrounding nations for their wickedness, promising justice to His people. His prophecy toward Judah was hopeful because God would purify and protect a remnant of those who remained faithful. Zephaniah pointed toward a day when God would bring them back from captivity, save them, delight in them, and rejoice over them. Despite their sin, His steadfast love remained.

Zephaniah reminds us that God's love demands His justice. The destruction He allowed was for their good, to draw their hearts back to Him. And even in their suffering, they had hope that He was bringing renewal and purity among them for His glory. God can use everything we go through to draw us closer to Him when our hearts are surrendered to Him and we trust in His goodness and love.

. . . .

*"The LORD is in your midst, a mighty one
who will save; he will rejoice over you with
gladness; he will quiet you with his love;
he will exult over you with loud singing."*

ZEPHANIAH 3:17

. . . .

JEREMIAH (640-580 BC)

Key Term: Rejected
Recipient: Judah, Pre-exile and during exile

Known as the "Weeping Prophet," Jeremiah was a priest in Judah who spent his entire life mourning over the state of God's people and calling them to repentance. He prophesied the fall of Judah to the Babylonian Empire and the exile of God's people into captivity for seventy years. Even though Jeremiah was faithful to proclaim God's Word, the people refused to repent, rejected his message, and persecuted him.

But Jeremiah's prophecy wasn't all negative. He also prophesied of Israel's return to the land, of their restoration and healing, of God's faithful love for His people, and of a new covenant God would make with them when He would put His law in their minds and on their hearts.

Jeremiah's prophecy continued throughout the fall of Judah and their captivity in Babylon in 586 BC, where he encouraged the Israelites to settle down and build houses in Babylon and to pray for their prosperity as it would in turn prosper them (Jeremiah 29:4-14). Daniel and his three friends are an example of those who settled in Babylon with faithful hearts toward God. And exactly seventy years later, King Cyrus of Persia issued the decree that they could return to their land. Jeremiah's faithful words demonstrated the heart of a faithful God.

Jeremiah reminds us that His desire is always for our good. He is faithful, just, merciful, and true. We can trust God's heart toward us.

. . . .

*"You will seek me and find me, when
you seek me with all your heart."*

JEREMIAH 29:13

. . . .

HABAKKUK (640-597 BC)

Key Term: Reminded
Recipient: Judah, Pre-exile

Habakkuk is unusual among the prophets because he didn't speak a message from God to the people; rather, he spoke to God about the people. Habakkuk cried out to God for justice and deliverance from the oppression of the people of Judah at the hands of the rich and powerful. Because God's people continued to rebel against His law, despite short times of revival under godly kings like Josiah, violence and injustice prevailed. Habakkuk pleaded with God to respond and intervene.

God responded that He was indeed at work, raising up the Babylonians as His tool of punishment against Judah. Habakkuk again cried out to God, knowing that more hardship would come to His people. But God responded that the righteous should live by faith. In other words, when judgment comes, those who are guilty will be punished; those who are innocent should trust Him. The Babylonians would also face His judgment for their part in Judah's suffering. Judah should trust in God and wait on Him to fulfill His plan for them.

This short book by a little-known prophet offers encouragement to us that God is sovereign, faithful, just, and good. Even when we don't understand His ways, we can trust His heart.

· ·

"Though the fig tree should not blossom, nor fruit be on the vines, the produce of the olive fail and the fields yield no food, the flock be cut off from the fold and there be no herd in the stalls, yet I will rejoice in the Lord; I will take joy in the God of my salvation"

LAMENTATIONS 3:17-18

· ·

LAMENTATIONS (586 BC)

Key Term: Broken

Recipient: Judah, during the siege of Jerusalem

Lamentations is believed to be the work of the prophet Jeremiah. Written as an acrostic poem, like some of the Psalms, each lament contains twenty-two verses, the number of letters in the Hebrew alphabet. It's a poem of sorrow and mourning because of the actual siege of Jerusalem in 586. God had sent many prophets to warn them, but they ignored His warnings and refused to repent. God kept His word and demonstrated His righteous judgment toward their rebellion and apostasy.

> *"But they kept mocking the messengers of God, despising his words and scoffing at his prophets, until the wrath of the LORD rose against his people, until there was no remedy"* (2 Chronicles 36:16).

The Babylonians had torn down the walls of Jerusalem, destroyed the temple, and captured the people. They had broken the covenant with God, and the people were left broken and destitute. The poem is not without hope, however. The writer called on God's compassion and faithfulness, reminding the reader to trust in God and wait for His salvation.

Lamentations reminds us that even in times of God's discipline, His love never fails. He disciplines those He loves (Heb. 12:6). All sin has consequences, but God will allow those circumstances to draw our hearts to repentance and trust in Him.

• •

*"Because of the Lord's great love
we are not consumed, for his compassions
never fail. They are new every morning;
great is your faithfulness."*

LAMENTATIONS 3:22-23

• •

THE EXILE
Prophets

OBADIAH (605-570 BC)

Key Term: Doomed
Recipient: Edom/other nations

This short prophetic book was most likely written after the fall of Judah to Babylon. Not much information exists about Obadiah, and the date is disputed, but the prophecy itself is clear. The prophecy was directed not at Israel, but at another nation, reminding the reader that God is the Lord of all nations and holds all people accountable for their sins. God spoke through Obadiah that He would destroy Edom for attacking His people, and they eventually fell as a nation.

The Edomites were the descendants of Esau, who sold his birthright and did not inherit the covenant promises of Abraham. In their pride, they opposed God and his people, and God announced judgment on them as a nation. The prophet also proclaimed judgment on other nations that had opposed Israel. This message was hopeful for the people of Israel who had suffered much at the hands of other nations. While Israel's rebellion and rejection of God's ways had led to the destruction they had faced, God's mercy and lovingkindness toward them were evident in His judgment toward those other nations. Israel would be avenged for the suffering they had endured.

Obadiah teaches us that God is sovereign over all nations, and He is perfectly just in all His ways. Edom fell because they rejected God. Sin always leads to destruction, which is a reminder of our need for a Savior.

· ·

"Saviors shall go up to Mount Zion to rule Mount Esau, and the kingdom shall be the LORD's."

OBADIAH 21

· ·

DANIEL (605-530 BC)

Key Term: Faithful
Recipient: Judah, in exile

Daniel is an example of those who were faithful during the Babylonian captivity. The first few chapters are a historical narrative of Daniel and his friends living in exile in Babylon. Even those who love God and are faithful to Him suffer when a nation turns from God. But Daniel and his friends were examples of integrity and obedience to God's Word in a time of suffering.

When Jeremiah prophesied about the 70-year Babylonian captivity, God told the people to settle in Babylon, to build homes and marry and continue to make lives for themselves because He would preserve a remnant who would return to the Promised Land (Jeremiah 29:4-14). Daniel's faithfulness is an example of how to live for God during times of national apostasy. Daniel experienced the blessing and deliverance of God because of his faithfulness. The Lord blessed him and used him to interpret dreams, but he also experienced persecution.

The remaining chapters of Daniel are details of his visions from God. Daniel's dream of four beasts symbolized the world empires rising and falling—Babylon, Persia, Greece, and Rome. Babylon was the current empire that had been used by God as judgment for Judah's failure to keep the covenant. Persia was the coming empire that would take over, allowing the Jews to return to their land. Greece was a coming empire that would establish a common language, allowing the gospel to travel throughout the known world, and Rome was the future empire that would reign at the time of Jesus.

Daniel also prophesied of the Son of Man who would come, the "Anointed One" (Daniel 9:25). While some of his visions are difficult to understand, especially of the timing of events, they remind us that God is sovereign over all nations and that Jesus' kingdom reigns over all. Daniel teaches us to be faithful to God no matter what because we ultimately belong to His kingdom and not the kingdoms of this world.

*"'And to him was given dominion
and glory and a kingdom, that all peoples,
nations, and languages should serve him; his
dominion is an everlasting dominion, which
shall not pass away, and his kingdom
one that shall not be destroyed.'"*

DANIEL 7:14

EZEKIEL (593-565 BC)

Key Term: Forsaken
Recipient: Judah, in exile

Ezekiel was a priest who prophesied to Judah both before and during the exile using images, symbols, and parables that are strange to us. He described the glory of the Lord in fascinating symbolism, even as the glory departed the temple, fulfilling the vision of Micah. He prophesied the siege of Jerusalem and the destruction of the temple, describing the events using extended metaphors and imagery. God called Ezekiel to physically demonstrate some of the imagery for the people to visualize the consequences of their sin, yet they refused to repent.

Ezekiel was primarily concerned with the idolatry and apostasy of the people who had forsaken God's Word and rejected His covenant. He condemned the false prophets, idolatrous leaders, and faithless flock of Israel. Ezekiel mourned for the state of the people and the destruction God allowed as the consequence of their rebellion.

Still, God spoke through Ezekiel His plan to redeem His people, to give them a new heart and a new spirit (Ezekiel 11:19-20). Again in Chapter 37, in the famous "Valley of Dry Bones," God spoke a message of restoration and hope to His people. He would resurrect them and breathe His life and Spirit into them, and they would return to their land.

God's promise of "my servant David" who would be their King is a reminder to us today that His Word is true and faithful. Ezekiel ends with the vision of a new temple and the return of God's glory, ushering in a new era of redemption and restoration for God's people.

Ezekiel is somewhat difficult to read and understand, but it teaches us that God is holy and sin is serious. But it also reminds us that in Christ, we have been given new hearts and a new Spirit, transformed and filled with His power.

"'And I will give them one heart and a new spirit I will put within them. I will remove the heart of stone from their flesh and give them a heart of flesh, that they may walk in my statutes and keep my rules and obey them.'"

EZEKIEL 11:19-20

THE POST-EXILE Prophets

HAGGAI (520 BC)

Key Term: Encouraged
Recipient: Judah, post-exile

Haggai prophesied during the time of Ezra, so comparing these two books is helpful. The "second year of Darius" dates the work to 520 BC (Haggai 1:1). The Jews had been allowed to return to Jerusalem and rebuild under the leadership of Zerubbabel and Joshua, the high priest. Those who had returned, however, were busy building their own homes first. The prophet encouraged them to consider why they had yet to prosper: His house was still in ruins (1:9). God's temple was where sacrifices for sin were made and where God mediated His relationship with His people. Rebuilding the temple was the first step in restoring their covenant relationship with God. So they obeyed the Lord and got to work repairing the temple.

When the people became discouraged because it paled in comparison to the magnificence of Solomon's temple, God encouraged them to be obedient and continue the work, because His Spirit was with them. He declared the latter glory of that temple would be greater than its former glory (2:9). That prophecy was fulfilled when Mary and Joseph presented their Baby according to the Law of Moses (Luke 2:22-32). The Glory had returned to the temple.

Haggai reminds us that God calls us to work and service for His kingdom, and He empowers us with new hearts and the Holy Spirit to do so.

"'Work, for I am with you, declares the LORD of hosts, according to the covenant I made with you when you came out of Egypt. My Spirit remains in your midst. Fear not'"

HAGGAI 2:4b-5

ZECHARIAH (518 BC)

Key Term: Kept
Recipient: Judah, post-exile

A contemporary of Haggai, Zechariah was a prophet and a priest who prophesied to Judah after their return to the land. It had been nearly twenty years since the people had been allowed to return, but the temple work had not been completed because of opposition and discouragement. God called the people to return to Him, and He would return to them. In a series of visions, Zechariah reminded the people of their sinful past, their exile, and the hope of future restoration for Jerusalem and God's people. He urged the people to trust God and remain faithful to the work to which they had been called.

God declared that peace and prosperity were coming for His people, as well as judgment on Israel's enemies. The last six chapters focus on the coming King of Zion from the house of David, who would come into Jerusalem on a donkey, speak peace, and bring salvation, yet be pierced. But another day is coming in which He will return as King over all the earth.

Just as these words of prophecy brought hope to the people living in exile, they bring hope to us today that Jesus will return and reign forever.

- -

"'Rejoice greatly, O daughter of Zion! Shout aloud, O daughter of Jerusalem! Behold, your king is coming to you; righteous and having salvation is he, humble and mounted on a donkey, on a colt, the foal of a donkey.'"

ZECHARIAH 9:9

- -

MALACHI (425 BC)

Key Term: Challenged
Recipient: Judah, post-exile

Written about one hundred years after their return from captivity, Malachi presented several oracles or messages from God to the people. While they had returned to the land and rebuilt the temple, they still had not been faithful to the Lord and His covenant. They were not living as if they were God's chosen people.

Malachi defended God's love for Israel. He rebuked the priests for impure offerings. He rebuked the people for unfaithfulness. And He promised a messenger, one like Elijah, who would come and prepare the way before Him. Matthew identifies John the Baptist as the fulfillment of this messenger who prepared the way for Jesus. Malachi's prophecy was a call to return to their God who would come to them with healing in His wings. His voice was the last prophetic message to Israel for four hundred years until John the Baptist announced that the kingdom of God had come (Matt. 11:10-14).

Malachi reminds us that we all fall short of God's glory and need a Savior. Israel would not remain faithful to God in their own strength. They needed the coming King who would save them from their sins and empower them with His Spirit to live a life of consistent faithfulness to God. And so do we.

· ·

"'Behold, I send my messenger, and he will prepare the way before me. And the Lord whom you seek will suddenly come to his temple; and the messenger of the covenant in whom you delight, behold, he is coming, says the LORD of hosts.'"

MALACHI 3:1

· ·

The Intertestamental Period

The Silent Years

THE
Intertestamental
PERIOD

The intertestamental period is the four hundred years between the Old Testament and the New Testament in which we do not have any canonical books. This period is sometimes called the silent years because no prophet spoke during these centuries, but much was happening politically, religiously, and culturally in the Middle East. We have other historical documents that reveal the events during these four hundred years, and they provide the context for the New Testament, mainly the writings of the Jewish historian Josephus.

This historical and cultural context is important for helping us situate the people and events in the New Testament, especially in the Gospels. In this section, we will explore the empires of the Middle East, the notable writings of that period, and the different cultural and social groups that formed.

EMPIRES OF THE INTERTESTAMENTAL PERIOD

EMPIRES	DATES	MAJOR LEADERS
The Persian Period	450-330 BC	Cyrus, Darius, Xerxes, Artaxerxes
The Greek (Hellenistic) Period	330-166 BC	Alexander the Great, Ptolemy, Seleucus, Antiochus
The Hasmonean (Jewish Independence) Period	166-63 BC	Mattathias and Judas Maccabeus
The Roman Period	63 BC-AD 476	Pompey, Julius Caesar, Octavian (Augustus)

Our English Bible closes the Old Testament with Malachi's prophecy, during which time the Persian Empire controlled Palestine, and the Jewish people were scattered throughout the land. Some of the

Jews returned to Israel under the edict of Cyrus, king of Persia. They had begun to rebuild and restore worship, yet Malachi reminds us that they still did not fully return to the Lord with all their heart. Many more Jews continued to live outside of Palestine, the name given to the land after Israel was exiled and other nations replanted there. Those scattered Jews are known as the Jews of the Diaspora, many of them having been born in exile where they assimilated into the cultures where they were.

Synagogue worship sprang up during this time as many of the Jewish people no longer had access to the temple. They began to meet in local places for prayer and reading of the Torah.

The Persian Empire soon gave way to the Greek Empire as Alexander the Great, a powerful military leader, conquered the Persians and took control of the land. He introduced Hellenistic or Greek culture throughout this region, with its emphasis on philosophy, education, and theater. By far the most important contribution of the Greek Empire was the Greek language, which became a second-known language to most in the region, paving the way for the spread of the Gospel to many different cultures.

When Alexander the Great died, his empire was split into four parts, led by his generals. Two of them, Ptolemy and Seleucus, battled for power over the region of Palestine. Ptolemy ended up ruling over Egypt which controlled Judea at that time. He gave the Jews a measure of freedom, not considering them a threat. His descendants that continued to rule the region after him let the Jews do what they wanted as long as they paid taxes and maintained peace.

Many of the Jews who lived outside Judea began to migrate to other communities. That Hellenistic culture grew and influenced them, eroding Jewish culture. For those traditional Jews, who knew they weren't holding to those foundational things that God had put into place, this influence became a concern.

The other general, Seleucus, controlled Syria. His descendants eventually attempted to gain Palestine. Under Antiochus III, the Seleucids defeated Egypt, and Palestine fell under Syrian control. Greek culture overtook Jerusalem as theaters, gymnasiums, and pagan events became the norm. Jewish priests were replaced with appointees by the government. Finally, in an attempt to gain complete control, Antiochus sent an army to impose paganism on the Jews. Jerusalem was ransacked, the temple was looted, and Judaism outlawed. Circumcision, reading the scrolls, celebrating the festivals, keeping the Sabbath—all those things were illegal under Seleucid control. Many Jewish men were killed, and women and children were enslaved. An altar to Zeus was erected in the temple and the worship of Zeus became mandatory.

In 167 BC a group of Jews led by Judas Maccabeus and his brothers revolted. They resisted Hellenistic culture and the Syrian oppressors, defeating them, regaining and cleansing the temple, and restoring worship. The Maccabean Revolt ushered in a period of Jewish independence known as the Hasmonean Dynasty or Maccabean Period. They inaugurated the festival of lights, the modern-day celebration known as Hanukah.

This revolt also led to a struggle for power between those who assimilated into that Hellenistic culture and those who wanted to hold onto the traditional Jewish culture. Meanwhile, the Roman Empire was beginning to expand under General Pompey. When these two groups vying for power turned to Rome for help, Pompey settled the conflict by taking over Jerusalem. Twelve thousand Jews died in a one-day siege. The Jewish rulers were divided between loyalty to their Jewish culture and allegiance to Rome out of a desire for self-preservation. Some of them wanted to resist but were afraid, so there was some quiet resistance. Some wanted to restore their Jewish culture, and Judaism split into different factions.

Some good things happened under the Roman Empire: Roads were built, commerce was strengthened, and the empire grew as the *Pax Romana* or Roman Peace spread. But it was a false peace created by subduing the people. Rome wanted to keep the peace, so they quickly put down any rebellion or strife. The Romans allowed natives to rule under them, so in the province of Judea, they appointed Herod the Great as king. He wasn't a Jew; he was an Edomite puppet of Rome. And he was evil, which made the Jews hate him even more. But he led many great building projects, such as a beautification project of the temple, which was in great disarray by this time. He had it restored to a magnificent structure to appease the people and maintain control over the Jews and good relations with Rome. The New Testament starts with the birth of Jesus in this time of uneasy tension, factions, and Roman oppression.

In this next section, we are going to look at some of the writings that developed during this time and contribute to our understanding of the historical and cultural context of the New Testament.

WRITINGS OF THE INTERTESTAMENTAL PERIOD

Apocrypha

The Apocrypha is a series of writings from this period, including some historical works, some fictional works, and some wisdom writings. They were included in the Septuagint, which was a Greek translation of the Hebrew Old Testament, but they were never considered part of the canon of OT Scripture. They do, however, give us important information about Judaism and culture in the Intertestamental Period.

Pseudepigrapha

The term Pseudepigrapha means "false signature" and refers to some extra-biblical writings outside the Bible. Some were claimed to have been authored by biblical figures, but none of them hold up under scrutiny. Historically and culturally they are important, however, because they give us insight into how varied the thinking of the Jews had become and how much Hellenistic influence had infiltrated their culture.

Dead Sea Scrolls

The Dead Sea Scrolls are from this time as well. They were discovered in the last century in a cave in the Qumran community, inhabited by the Essenes. There are 800 manuscripts, including commentaries on the Old Testament and copies of the OT Scriptures such as Isaiah, Psalms, and Deuteronomy. These copies verified the validity of the copies we already had, making this one of the most significant archaeological finds of the twentieth century.

Writings of Philosophers and Historians

We have the writings of Jewish scholars, such as commentaries on the OT, and historians, such as Josephus. Josephus was a Jewish historian during this period who chronicled the Jewish war with Rome and gave us much of the historical context of the Intertestamental Period. Philo of Alexandria was a Jewish philosopher whose writings from Egypt give us some understanding of the lives of Jews of the Diaspora (living outside Palestine) during the first century.

Septuagint

The Greek translation of the Hebrew Old Testament, the Septuagint (sometimes referred to as LXX) was of major importance as Greek became the second language of the known world.

SOCIAL GROUPS IN CONFLICT IN THE INTERTESTAMENTAL PERIOD[23]

Temple: in Jerusalem, place of sacrificial worship system, Jewish ceremonies	**Synagogue:** local houses of worship for reading of Torah, traditional way of life
Sadducees: aligned with the temple; sought position with Rome	**Pharisees:** aligned with the synagogues; sought approval of the people
Sanhedrin: formed during the Greek Empire as a Jewish civil council with the high priest of the temple as the head	**Scribes:** held to a more traditional way of life of the people
Herodians: Jews who connected with Roman aristocracy and would compromise to hold onto their status, power, and wealth	**Essenes:** wanted to separate from Roman culture; withdrew to separate communities
Publicans: dregs of Jewish society loyal to Rome (tax collectors)	**Zealots:** extreme religious radicals leftover from the Maccabean revolt

These different groups conflicted over Jewish sovereignty and worship. Some wanted to compromise with their culture and assimilated into Roman life; others wanted to separate from or fight against Rome, preserving traditional Jewish values and culture.

The temple had been rebuilt under Ezra but then was desecrated under Antiochus III. It was later restored and beautified under Herod during the Roman Empire, so by the first century, worship had been restored at the temple, but the Jews that were scattered had begun to worship in their local synagogues. Those aligned with the temple were holding to the ceremonial sacrifices from the Old Testament. Those aligned with the synagogues were not making sacrifices, but they were very devoted to the Word of God and the traditional way of life.

The Sadducees presided over the temple, and the Pharisees ruled in the synagogues. The Sadducees only used the Law of Moses as their Scriptures and didn't believe in angels, resurrection, or the afterlife. The Pharisees used the entire Old Testament, but they had added to the OT Laws and sought to uphold all those commands to the letter.

The Sanhedrin was the Jewish ruling council, like a civil court that developed during the time of the Greek Empire. The high priest of the temple was the head of the Sanhedrin. The scribes were

---

[23] Bert Downs, *Bible Survey: A Big Screen Perspective,* BiblicalTraining.org, 2020.

teachers of the Law who were from among the Pharisees and the synagogue. They held to the more traditional way of life of the people.

The Herodians were wealthy Jews who wanted to stay on the good side of the aristocracy of Rome because it gave them wealth and power and position. So they aligned themselves with Herod, Rome's puppet, and were most likely political patrons.

The Essenes were separatists who refused to compromise with Gentile culture, so they withdrew and lived in separate communities. They were pious, monk-like Jews who kept very strict discipline and purity laws. The Qumran community where the Dead Sea Scrolls were found was probably an Essene commune.

The publicans were lower-class citizens aligned with Rome for their security and well-being. Most Jews did not like them because they often cheated their people. They extorted money when they were collecting taxes and kept it for themselves.

The zealots, also known as the "Fourth Philosophy" were rebels who were willing to fight to be freed from Roman occupation. Their resistance was based on the fact that the Maccabean revolt had freed them from Syrian oppression, so they knew it was possible.

The New Testament begins amid this historical and cultural context. The first-century culture of Judea was a time of political unrest, social turmoil, and religious confusion and division. No prophet had spoken in four hundred years, and hope seemed dim to most. Understanding this context and the different groups and how strongly they held to their own beliefs helps us to better understand much of the reactions to Jesus and others in the Gospels.

The New

Testament

"And the Word became flesh and dwelt among us..."
John 1:14a

The Gospels

Yeshua

THE
Gospels

The word *gospel* means "good news" or "announcement." After four hundred years of prophetic silence, John the Baptist emerged from the wilderness with good news: the kingdom of heaven is near. The first four books of the New Testament—Matthew, Mark, Luke, and John—were written as historical narratives with theological implications. They may be considered biographies of the life of Christ, but not in the modern sense of a biography that seeks to tell someone's personal life story from beginning to end. The Gospels do not give us the complete life of Christ from birth to ascension. Most of Jesus' life is left out. Instead, the Gospels focus mainly on eyewitness accounts of roughly three years of His life and ministry so that people may believe that He was the Messiah prophesied by Israel's God in the Old Testament.

Luke began his account with his reason for writing:

> *"Inasmuch as many have undertaken to compile a narrative of the things that have been accomplished among us, just as those who from the beginning were eyewitnesses and ministers of the word have delivered them to us, it seemed good to me also, having followed all things closely for some time past, to write an orderly account for you, most excellent Theophilus, that you may have certainty concerning the things you have been taught" (Luke 1:1-4).*

Likewise, John explicitly states his reason for penning his Gospel account:

> *"Now Jesus did many other signs in the presence of the disciples, which are not written in this book; but these are written so that you may believe that Jesus is the Christ, the Son of God, and that by believing you may have life in his name" (John 20:30-31).*

The first three Gospels (Matthew, Mark, and Luke) are what we call the synoptic gospels. Synoptic means "seeing together." These three can be "seen together" as telling the same basic stories because much of their content is the same. John shares different content (90% of John is not found in the other Gospels[24]) that does not contradict but complements the first three Gospels.

So, why do we have four different accounts of the life of Christ in the Bible written by four different authors? Well, each evangelist (Gospel writer) gives us a little different perspective on the events that took place. All four of them together provide a richer and fuller picture of what Jesus' life and teachings were like. Each of them presents a different aspect of who Jesus was and is. Scholars call this presentation of Jesus the writer's Christology.

When we read the Gospels, we are separated from the original audience by time, language, geography, and culture. Learning to read the New Testament in light of its time and place will help to better understand its meaning. Three important aspects of Middle Eastern culture are honor/ shame, community, and hospitality. Whereas we in the West view actions as right or wrong, their culture sees them through the lens of honor or shame. Because they are community-oriented rather than individualistic as we are, they place great emphasis upon what brings shame or honor to not only the family but also the entire community. And to show hospitality is a source of honor; whereas, to fail to show hospitality is a source of shame.

Understanding these cultural differences will help us begin to read the Gospels through the lens of their worldview rather than our own. In the appendix, I have listed some books that will further your understanding of first-century Middle Eastern culture.

The consensus of most biblical scholars is that Mark was written first, followed by Matthew and Luke who probably used some of the material in Mark. John was written later toward the end of the first century. Understanding each of the authors, their backgrounds and perspectives, and their audiences can help us better comprehend their words.

A horizontal view of the four Gospels gives us an overall picture of the life and ministry of Jesus Christ by comparing all four accounts and assimilating them into one cohesive narrative. A vertical approach allows us to read each Gospel separately to get a deeper understanding of the unique perspective of the evangelist.

---

[24] Mark L. Strauss, *Four Portraits, One Jesus: A Survey of Jesus and the Gospels* (Grand Rapids: Zondervan, 2007), 298.

HORIZONTAL VIEW OF
the Life of Christ

The Israelites were a nation chosen by God to know and worship Him, brought into covenant with Him, and given commands that would set them apart from other nations as people who worshiped God alone and loved and honored their neighbor. But over the years, they rejected God and his law.

He sent prophets to warn them of coming judgment, but also to call them back to a relationship with Him, promising that He would one day send a descendant of their great King David, who would bring salvation and deliverance to all the world.

Jesus of Nazareth was the fulfillment of that prophecy. He was a Jew who lived in the first century in Palestine which was under the control of the Roman Empire at that time. He was miraculously conceived by the Holy Spirit to a young girl called Mary, who was a virgin and betrothed to a carpenter named Joseph, a descendant of King David. Jesus was born around 6-4 BC in the small town of Bethlehem.

His public ministry began when he was around 30 in the area of Galilee. He taught that the kingdom of God had arrived, calling people to repent of their sins and believe in Him. Crowds followed Him as He performed miracles witnessed by many—healing the lame, blind, and deaf, and casting out demons.

His teachings were based on the OT laws of the Jews, but He interpreted them differently from the religious leaders of the day who had added their own traditions and interpretations. Jesus claimed to be the Son of God, the fulfillment of the OT law, and to have the authority to interpret it accurately. He forgave sins, walked on water, raised the dead, and revealed the heart of God to people. He called his followers to a life of love for God and other people, service, humility, and persecution.

The religious leaders began to question and challenge his claims to authority, accusing him of blasphemy. They eventually sought to kill Him by having the Roman authorities convict Him of treason since they had no authority to execute. He began to prepare His followers for His execution on a Roman cross which was all part of God's plan, that He would die as a sacrifice for the sins of the world so that all sinful people could be in a relationship with a holy God.

He was arrested and tried before both Jewish and Roman officials: the Jewish trial for blasphemy, and the Roman trial for treason. Although the Roman governor at the time, Pontius Pilate, found no grounds for the accusations, out of fear, he handed Jesus over to be crucified. His followers buried Him in a tomb before the start of the Sabbath. When the day of rest was over, some of His followers went to the tomb and found it empty, encountering an angel who declared He had risen!

After that, He appeared alive to many people, over 500, for 40 days. After commissioning His followers to proclaim His teachings and make disciples of all the nations, He was taken back up into heaven right before their eyes. His followers continued to worship Him and proclaim His coming and His teaching, and many more became His disciples. Eyewitnesses recorded these events while other historians and writers also acknowledged these truths about who Jesus was.

MARK

Author: John Mark, cousin of Barnabas, missionary, and companion of Peter and Paul
Date: AD 40-60
Recipients: Gentiles
Christology: Suffering Servant
Key Theme: Jesus came to go to the cross

Mark's Gospel is the shortest and most fast-paced of the four. Early historical documents show that Mark was a close associate of Peter and preserved the preaching of Peter and the oral traditions about the life of Jesus. Many of the individual accounts are from Peter's perspective as one who was in Jesus' inner circle. Since Mark explains Jewish customs to his readers and interprets Aramaic words, it is assumed that his audience was primarily Gentile, probably Roman.

Mark presented Jesus as the Suffering Servant of Isaiah 53, always pointing toward the cross. It's been said that Mark's account is a passion story with an extended introduction because of his emphasis on the crucifixion.[25] In this account of Jesus' life, we get no genealogy, no birth narrative, no childhood account, no temptation of Christ, no Sermon on the Mount, and no cleansing of the temple. Mark focused more on the authority and actions of Jesus than on His teachings, which would have appealed to a Roman audience who understood the significance of authority. Those actions were always pointing toward the cross.

While Mark contains fewer narrative accounts than the other Gospels, he often included more details than the other Gospels. His account highlighted the reactions of people to Jesus' claim of authority as the Son of God and His role as the Servant who heals, comforts, and delivers.

---

[25] Robert Wayne Stacy, Video Lecture for NBST 515 (Liberty University, Lynchburg, VA, 2019).

Mark's Gospel reminds us of God's love for all people, not just the Jewish nation. And Mark points us to the authority and actions of Jesus that led people to either love Him or hate Him, reminding us today to search our hearts for how we respond to His authority in our lives.

. . . .

"And calling the crowd to him with his disciples, he said to them, 'If anyone would come after me, let him deny himself and take up his cross and follow me. For whoever would save his life will lose it, but whoever loses his life for my sake and the gospel's will save it.'"

MARK 8:34-35

. . . .

MATTHEW

Author: Matthew or Levi, tax collector, one of the Twelve Apostles
Date: before AD 70
Recipients: Jews
Christology: Messiah
Key Theme: Jesus is the fulfillment of OT prophecy

Matthew was a tax collector who worked for the Roman government. Tax collectors were considered traitors among the Jews because of their association with the oppressive government and because they often cheated their people, collecting more than was necessary and keeping it for themselves. Yet, Jesus called Matthew to follow Him, and he became a disciple of Christ. His Gospel is, therefore, a meticulous eyewitness account of the important events of Jesus' life, including His teaching, miracles, crucifixion, and resurrection.

Matthew's Gospel presented Jesus as the "new and greater Moses."[26] Written to a Jewish audience, Matthew's purpose was to prove that Jesus is the long-awaited Messiah of whom the OT prophesied. Just as Moses gave Israel the Torah—the first five books of the OT Law—Jesus gave five main discourses in which He taught what God intended through the Law. He came to fulfill the Law or give it full meaning. Like Moses, Jesus spoke these words from a mountain in the famous Sermon on the Mount. Matthew's Jewish audience would have understood the significance of this comparison with Moses.

Matthew began with a genealogy that reveals Jesus as the son of David and Abraham, both of these in fulfillment of OT prophecy. Matthew focused on and frequently referenced OT prophecies of the Messiah, demonstrating that Jesus was the fulfillment of them. A frequent term in Matthew's Gospel is the kingdom of God or Heaven, which he used multiple times. Matthew presented Jesus as the Jewish Messianic Hope who ushered in the kingdom of God, which was not the political and military triumph over Rome that many Jews expected but a spiritual reality where God reigns in the hearts and lives of His people.

Matthew's Gospel teaches us that Jesus is the fulfillment of the OT prophecies of the Messiah who would come to set us free from the bondage of sin and bring us into the eternal kingdom of God. We can learn what life in that kingdom looks like and how we should live our lives in light of our redemption.

---

[26] Robert H. Gundry, *A Survey of the New Testament,* 5th ed. (Grand Rapids: Zondervan, 2012), 188.

"And Jesus came and said to them. 'All authority in heaven and on earth has been given to me. Go therefore and make disciples of all nations, baptizing them in the name of the Father and of the Son and of the Holy Spirit, teaching them to observe all that I have commanded you. And behold, I am with you always, to the end of the age.'"

MATTHEW 28:18-20

LUKE

Author: Luke, a doctor, historian, and disciple of Paul
Date: AD 50-60
Recipients: Theophilus, Greeks, and Hellenistic Jews
Christology: Savior of All
Key Theme: humanity and compassion of Jesus to all people

Luke's beloved Gospel gives us the Christmas narrative with which we are so familiar. As a disciple of Paul, Luke tells us he carefully investigated all of the reports about Jesus and documented the evidence in this account. His role as an accurate historian has been noted by scholars as names, places, and dates have been verified through archaeology. Luke's profession as a doctor may explain his compassion for those whom society ignored—children, women, and the poor. His classical Greek writing style shows his level of education and Hellenistic influence, as well as the fact that his audience was most likely Greek Gentiles or at least Hellenistic Jews.

Luke presented Jesus as the Savior of all mankind, from his genealogy which begins with Adam to his emphasis on social outcasts. Luke alone shared the account of the immoral woman who anointed Jesus, the prodigal son, Zacchaeus, and the parable of the Good Samaritan. His Gospel emphasizes the role of women in the ministry of Jesus, such as Elizabeth, Anna, Mary, and Martha, the poor widow, and the women who supported Jesus financially, stayed near the cross, and witnessed the empty tomb. While Jesus was both fully divine and fully human in His incarnation, Luke stressed the humanity and compassion of Christ.

Luke's Gospel has more references to prayer and the Holy Spirit than the other Gospel accounts, which we see continued in his account of the early church in Acts. His birth narrative and passion narrative are both longer than that of other Gospels with Luke standing as the longest book in the NT. By his focus on Jesus as the Savior of all, Luke presented an account of the life of Christ that would appeal to Gentiles, Greeks, Romans, men, women, children, the poor, the outcasts, and all of society. Through Luke, God reveals Himself as the Savior of all mankind.

Luke's Gospel teaches us that God's love is for all people, regardless of nationality, gender, social status, economic status, or age. Luke's historic accuracy assures us of the reliability of the Gospel accounts, deepening our trust in God.

• •

*"'For the Son of Man came
to seek and to save the lost.'"*

LUKE 19:10

• •

JOHN

Author: John the "Beloved Disciple," fisherman, son of Zebedee, one of the Twelve Apostles
Date: AD 90's
Recipients: Christians in general
Christology: Son of God
Key Theme: the divinity of Jesus, dualism

John, brother of James and one of the Twelve Apostles, wrote the most spiritual and theological of the four Gospels. Describing himself as the "disciple whom Jesus loved," John experienced a close relationship with Jesus. He was a cousin of Jesus (His mother was Salome, the sister of Mary and wife of Zebedee.) John was a fisherman and one of Jesus' inner circle, along with James and Peter.

Because so much of the material in John is not found in the other three Gospels, it supplements much of the Synoptics. Written later in the century, the Gospel of John added details Matthew, Mark, and Luke did not include. As an eyewitness of events, John wrote during a time of persecution for Christians and emphasized the significance of Jesus as the divine Son of God in whom they should continue to trust.

While Luke stressed the humanity of Jesus, John stressed His divinity. He skipped the birth narratives that had already been recorded in Matthew and Luke, and began with the famous Logos (Word) prologue:

> *"In the beginning was the Word, and the Word was with God, and the Word was God. He was in the beginning with God" (John 1:1-2).*

With allusions to Creation, John described Jesus as the Word who has always existed but chose to become flesh and dwell among us as the glory of the Father. John used many contrasts, such as light/dark and life/death. He included the seven "I am" statements of Jesus that echo God's revelation to Moses as the "I Am" or Yahweh.

- I am the Bread of Life

- I am the Light of the World

- I am the Door

- I am the Good Shepherd

- I am the Resurrection and the Life

- I am the Way, the Truth, and the Life

- I am the True Vine

John focused on the miraculous events and powerful statements of Jesus that caused the Jewish religious leaders to charge Him with blasphemy. His claim to be God is what led to His execution, and John wanted to remind believers of that fact since they were undergoing persecution and may have been tempted to doubt. John affirmed Jesus' divinity by selecting narratives that demonstrated the miracles, signs, statements, and works of Jesus that reveal His glory as the divine Son of God so that all the world may believe in Him and have eternal life (30:31).

John's Gospel teaches us that Jesus truly was and is the divine Son of God who calls us out of darkness and into His light. Because He was truly God and truly man, Jesus has the power to save us and give us life in His name.

. . . .

"Jesus said to him, 'I am the way, and the truth, and the life. No one comes to the Father except through me.'"

JOHN 14:6

. . . .

The Acts

Holy Spirit

THE ACTS OF THE
Apostles

Timeline: about AD 30-60

Theme: Historical account of the early church

Author: Luke, a doctor, historian, and disciple of Paul

Date: AD 63

The book of Acts can best be described as "theological history—a narrative of interrelated events from a given place and time, chosen to communicate theological truths."[27] It is a continuation of Luke's Gospel, written specifically to Theophilus, as Luke stated in his introduction:

> *"In the first book, O Theophilus, I have dealt with all that Jesus began to do and teach, until the day when he was taken up, after he had given commands through the Holy Spirit to the apostles whom he had chosen" (Acts 1:1-2).*

Luke then continued the historical account of the early church after Jesus' ascension into heaven. So, while Acts presents a history of the Christian faith, it also shows the power of the Holy Spirit at work in the lives of those who spread the gospel message in the first decades of the church amid opposition and persecution.

Because of Luke's attention to detail and historical accuracy, Acts provides an in-depth description of the witness of the believers, especially Paul, as the church grew beyond Jerusalem and Judea. Through the sermons, witness, and teachings of the disciples and the missionary journeys of Paul and his companions, which at times included Luke, Acts reveals the theological development of the early church. From the dramatic conversion of Paul on the road to Damascus to the arrests, martyrdom, and supernatural events that took place, Acts is one of the most exciting and powerful books in the Bible.

---

[27] William W. Klein, Craig L. Blomberg, and Robert L. Hubbard, Jr., *Introduction to Biblical Interpretation,* 3rd. ed. (Grand Rapids: Zondervan, 2017), 532.

Much like the Gospels, Acts must be interpreted in light of both aspects of the genre—both historically and theologically. As a historical narrative, Acts follows the progression of Acts 1:8—the Holy Spirit empowered the disciples to be witnesses in Jerusalem (Ch. 1-7), Judea and Samaria (Ch. 8-9), and to the ends of the earth (Ch. 10-28).

In Jerusalem

- Ascension 40 days after the resurrection, Pentecost, Holy Spirit empowers believers

- Peter's sermon, imprisonment of Peter and John

- Miracles, conversions, persecution

- Martyrdom of Stephen

In Judea and Samaria

- Philip in Samaria

- Ethiopian eunuch

- Conversion of Saul

Beyond Judea and Samaria

- Cornelius and Peter's vision

- Gospel goes to Antioch, the first church community

- Execution of James and imprisonment of Peter

- Paul's missionary journeys

- Events in Jerusalem

- Riot and Paul's arrest, defense before the Sanhedrin

- Plot to kill Paul, his transfer to Caesarea

- The trial before Felix, Festus, and appeal to Rome

- Voyage to Rome and shipwreck

- Paul preaching under house arrest in Rome

Luke ends with Paul under house arrest in Rome, most likely because it was written during that time. We don't get the end of that story because it had not happened yet. The work of the Holy Spirit in the life of the church continues today.

One way to study the book of Acts is to combine it with the study of Paul's letters chronologically. The historical and cultural context of the growth of the church and Paul's missionary journeys bring clarity to both Acts and the epistles.

The chart on the following page shows the approximate dating of Paul's letters in relation to his travels as outlined by Luke in Acts.

"But you will receive power when the Holy Spirit has come upon you, and you will be my witnesses in Jerusalem and in all Judea and Samaria, and to the end of the earth."

ACTS 1:8

THE ACTS & THE EPISTLES ALIGNED

As you read Acts, you will come to the places Paul was when he wrote the epistles. You can stop and study the epistles individually as you study the historical context in Acts.

ACTS

Chapters 1-14

Chapters 15-17

Chapters 18-19

Chapter 20

Chapters 21-28

EPISTLES

Galatians

1 Thessalonians
2 Thessalonians

1 Corinthians

2 Corinthians
Romans

Philemon
Colossians
Ephesians

Philippians
1 Timothy
Titus
2 Timothy

The Pauline
Epistles

Grace

THE PAULINE

Epistles

The Apostle Paul wrote thirteen of the twenty-seven books of the New Testament. They are all epistles or letters, written either to churches or to individuals. Much like Greco-Roman letters of the first century, they are structured with an introduction, body, and conclusion. Letters functioned as authoritative substitutes for the apostles to churches and individuals; they were written primarily to address situations, to clarify doctrine, or to confront particular behaviors; they were carefully composed and delivered by trusted carriers; and they were intended to be read aloud to the Christian community.[28]

First-century writers used letters to communicate because travel was slow and difficult. The apostles were not always able to address concerns or express encouragement in person, so letters were used to stay connected with the Christian communities and individuals they served. These authoritative letters were used to "apply theology in practical ways to specific situations in churches."[29] Therefore, when interpreting a NT letter, one must first consider the genre by reading through the entire letter from beginning to end without removing passages or verses from their literary context.

Then, because they address specific situations or occasions in the lives of the recipients, we should seek to understand the historical-cultural situation. Next, we should observe the author's flow of thought and the main point of each paragraph or passage. Last, we should then determine the timeless principles that are reflected in the text, that are not culturally bound, that are consistent with the rest of Scripture, and that are relevant to both the ancient and modern reader.[30] Identifying these particular nuances helps us to differentiate the author's original purpose and identify the theological principles for modern application.

---

[28] J. Scott Duvall and J. Daniel Hays, *Grasping God's Word: A Hands-On Approach to Reading, Interpreting, and Applying the Bible,* 4th ed. (Grand Rapids: Zondervan Academic, 2020), 259-263.

[29] Ibid., 260.

[30] Ibid., 267-271.

Understanding where these letters fall within the scope of the metanarrative of Scripture is also essential for gaining understanding. In the Creation-Fall-Redemption-Restoration paradigm, the NT letters are between redemption and complete restoration because Jesus has come and redeemed those who repent of their sins and put their trust in Him. The restoration of all things will not be complete, however, until Christ's return; so we live in what scholars call the "already-not-yet" era of church history. We are already redeemed and justified before the Father, but we are in the process of sanctification, or being conformed to the likeness of Christ. Therefore, many of the NT letters include instructions about how to live out the principles Jesus taught as we await our final redemption.

As mentioned in the last section, reading Paul's letters in light of his missionary journeys outlined in Acts can bring clarity to the historical, cultural, and situational context of each letter. Another chart on the next page gives a fuller picture of how his letters fit into the context of his travels as Paul carried the gospel to the Gentiles.

PAUL'S MISSIONS & EPISTLES

On the left is an outline of the places Paul visited on his missionary journeys according to Acts. On the right is the approximate timing of the letters he wrote as determined by scholars.

JOURNEYS

outlined in Acts

LETTERS

approximate time of writing

Journeys	Letters
A.D. 34 Paul's conversion, time in Damascus, visit to Jerusalem, return to Tarsus, and visit to Antioch (Syria)	
47 Barnabas & Paul deliver offering to Jerusalem	
1st missionary journey: Cyprus, Perga, Antioch (Pisidia), Iconium, Lystra, Derbe, and back to Antioch (Syria)	
49 The Jerusalem Council	Galatians
50-51 **2nd missionary journey**: Derbe, Lystra, Iconium, Antioch (Pisidia), Troas, Philippi, Thessalonica, Berea, Athens, Corinth, Cenchrea, Ephesus, Caesarea, Jerusalem, and back to Antioch (Syria).	1 & 2 Thessalonians (from Corinth)
3rd missionary journey: Galatia, Ephesus, Philippi, Thessalonica, Berea, Greece, Macedonia, Troas, Miletus, Tyre, Caesarea, Jerusalem, Caesarea **57**	1 Corinthians (from Ephesus) 2 Corinthians (from Macedonia) Romans (from Greece)
60 **Journey to Rome**: Caesarea, Crete, Malta	Philemon Colossians Ephesians
61 Rome under house arrest	Philippians
63 Released from prison, further traveling	1 Timothy & Titus 2 Timothy
Reimprisonment Martyrdom	

LETTERS OF Paul

Letters during his missionary journeys:

- Galatians

- 1 and 2 Thessalonians

- 1 & 2 Corinthians

- Romans

Prison letters written while under house arrest in Rome

- Philemon

- Colossians

- Ephesians

- Philippians

Pastoral letters written during a brief release from prison before 2nd imprisonment and martyrdom

- 1 Timothy

- Titus

- 2 Timothy (probably written during his 2nd imprisonment, shortly before his death)

The letters of Paul show us how the early church lived out the life and teachings of Christ amid persecution, false teachers, and the spread of a global gospel for all people.

GALATIANS

Date: AD 49, after Paul's 1st missionary journey
Place of writing: Antioch in Syria
Recipients: Christians in Psidian Antioch, Iconium, and Lystra (South Galatia)
Themes: Justification by faith

Paul wrote the letter to the Galatians to address division in the church over Jewish customs. The church consisted of both Jewish and Gentile converts. Some false teachers called Judaizers had convinced many of the believers that Jewish customs and ceremonies had to be followed to be saved. Paul refuted that teaching by proclaiming the gospel of Christ which is justification by faith alone.

Paul established his authority as an apostle of Christ Jesus first. He then addressed the Judaizing controversy by proclaiming the gospel of Jesus Christ. The OT ceremonial laws for Israel, such as circumcision and the purity laws about certain foods were to set them apart from other nations. These were part of the covenant God made with Abraham, pointing toward the need for the Savior who was to come.

Jesus fulfilled the old covenant and established the new covenant in His blood. Followers of Christ do not have to become Jews to be saved. Salvation is not the result of works of the law but of faith in Jesus' finished work on the cross. That is the essence of the gospel. Paul refuted the false teaching of those who demanded circumcision for Gentile believers. He reminded them they had been filled with the Holy Spirit and given freedom in Christ to live and walk by the Spirit, bearing fruit for God's glory.

Galatians is a reminder to us that we cannot earn salvation through outward behaviors. Our good works are simply our response of love and gratitude to God and the working of His Spirit within us.

. . . .

*"For in Christ Jesus neither circumcision
nor uncircumcision counts for anything,
but only faith working through love."*

GALATIANS 5:6

. . . .

1 & 2 THESSALONIANS

Date: AD 50-51, during 2nd missionary journey
Place of writing: Corinth
Recipients: Christians in Thessalonica
Theme: Christian growth; the second coming of Christ

First Thessalonians was written to believers who were enduring persecution for their beliefs. Acts 17 provides the context for these letters. Paul wrote to encourage the Christians and remind them that they do not grieve without hope. He urged them to continue in the faith with joy, gratitude, and prayer, trusting in Jesus who is faithful.

Paul wrote 2 Thessalonians to continue to encourage them in the face of persecution and also to refute false teaching that the day of the Lord had already happened. Paul explained that Jesus' return would occur after a great falling away and the appearance of the Antichrist, whom Jesus will defeat. He reassured the believers that this day had not yet arrived and rebuked those who were teaching false doctrine. Paul encouraged them to work hard for the Lord and to stand firm, holding to what they had been taught.

These letters encourage us today to put our hope in Jesus as we grieve, live, learn, and grow, standing on the truths of His Word. We, too, are instructed to not be led away by false teaching but to be firmly grounded in God's Word as we trust in and await Christ's return.

- -

"Now may our Lord Jesus Christ himself, and God our Father, who loved us and gave us eternal comfort and good hope through grace, comfort your hearts and establish them in every good work and word."

2 THESSALONIANS 2:17

- -

1 & 2 CORINTHIANS

Date: AD 55-56, during 3rd missionary journey
Place of writing: Ephesus; Macedonia
Recipients: Christians in Corinth
Theme: Divisions in church; encouragement

Paul wrote 1 Corinthians near the end of his three-year ministry in Ephesus. He had spent significant time in Corinth on his second missionary journey and was well-acquainted with the believers there. The believers were divided over their loyalties to different leaders in the church. Paul addressed their controversies by proclaiming Christ and His cross as the central unifying power of their faith. Paul addressed other issues in the church, such as sexual immorality, lawsuits, principles on marriage and singleness, and wisdom regarding their rights as believers. His instruction was to do what glorifies God and builds up others. Paul then gave instructions for church gatherings, including order for The Lord's Supper, the use of spiritual gifts, and the supremacy of love. He ends his letter with a reminder of the power of the resurrection, on which the whole of Christianity stands.

His letter's primary theme is the issue of Christian conduct within the church. He wrote to encourage the believers that the Gospel has the power to change their hearts and impact every part of their lives. These words have much to teach us today about how we live in light of Christ's life, death, and resurrection.

Paul later wrote 2 Corinthians from Macedonia to address some challenges to his authority as an apostle by some false teachers who had infiltrated the church. He defended his integrity, offered forgiveness, and acknowledged that his ministry was only to proclaim Christ and not himself. Therefore, he could endure opposition because he worked for an eternal glory. Paul proclaimed to them the ministry of reconciliation and himself as simply Christ's ambassador.

He then encouraged the believers to live pure lives with godly sorrow that leads to repentance. He inspired them to continue to be generous to the churches in Macedonia with their gifts, which he would collect when he next visited them.

Second Corinthians reminds us to keep Jesus at the center of our lives and ministry, to seek reconciliation with God and others, to give generously to kingdom work, and to not lose heart during times of suffering.

··

*"We are therefore Christ's ambassadors,
as though God were making his appeal
through us. We implore you on Christ's
behalf: Be reconciled to God."*

2 CORINTHIANS 5:20

··

ROMANS

Date: AD 57, during 3rd missionary journey
Place of writing: Corinth
Recipients: Christians in Rome
Theme: The Gospel; justification by grace through faith for Jew and Gentile

Paul wrote this letter from Corinth to the believers in Rome, a city he had yet to visit. The believers there were primarily Gentile, probably converts who had been in Jerusalem on the Day of Pentecost, as no apostle can be associated historically with establishing the gospel in Rome. The Jews had been expelled from Rome under Emperor Claudius in AD 49 or 50.[31] A few years later, after the death of Claudius, Jews had returned and possibly disrupted the unity of the churches there, by insisting that Gentiles obey the Law of Moses. Paul wrote this letter to prepare the believers there for his coming visit he hoped to make soon. Written almost as a theological essay, Paul outlined the basic truths of the gospel and God's plan of salvation for all the world—Jews and Gentiles alike.

Paul began with his plan to visit them and a statement that set the tone for the remainder of his letter: "I am not ashamed of the gospel, because it is the power of God for the salvation of everyone who believes: first for the Jew, then for the Gentile" (1:16). He then described the state of all people as sinful, both Jews and Gentiles. He proclaimed the death of Jesus as the substitutionary sacrifice for sin, justifying by grace those who put their faith in Him. He explained the failure of the Law to produce righteousness and the power of the Spirit to produce right living.

Paul then described the state of Israel's unbelief and future restoration for Israel. He encouraged the believers to live for God, to love one another, to avoid offending weaker Christians, and to be aware of false teachers in the church.

Romans is a great reminder to us today of the truth of the gospel message and its impact on our lives. Romans 8 is an encouragement to live with our hearts and minds set on the Spirit and not the sinful nature. Romans 12-16 provide practical instructions for how to actively live out the principles of the gospel in our everyday lives.

---

[31] Gundry, *A Survey of the NT,* 431.

··

*"There is therefore now no condemnation
for those who are in Christ Jesus. For the
law of the Spirit of life has set you free in
Christ Jesus from the law of sin and death."*

ROMANS 8:1-2

··

PHILEMON

Date: AD 61-62
Place of writing: Rome
Recipients: Philemon and his church in Colossae
Theme: Mercy and Reconciliation in Christ

Paul wrote this short letter, along with Ephesians, Philippians, and Colossians, together known as the Prison Epistles, while he was on house arrest in Rome awaiting trial before Caesar. While under house arrest, he had the freedom to have visitors and to write letters to encourage the faith and perseverance of the saints (Acts 28:16, 30). The letter is addressed to Philemon, a believer from Colossae, who had a slave named Onesimus. Apparently, Onesimus had stolen from Philemon and then run away but later heard the gospel from Paul and became a Christian. Because Onesimus could have faced the death penalty, Paul wrote to Philemon to plead for him to show mercy and accept Onesimus as a brother in Christ.

Paul's letter demonstrates the nature of the gospel of Jesus Christ. In Him, we are forgiven, so we show forgiveness. We have received mercy, so we should show mercy. Jesus taught these principles in the Sermon on the Mount, and Paul wanted to teach the entire church in Colossae that these principles are meant to be lived out in our daily actions and relationships with others.

Paul sent the letter with Onesimus and Tychicus, along with the letter to the Colossians and a lost letter to the Laodicean believers (Col. 4:16). The letters were intended to be read aloud in church and circulated to the other churches as well. His message to Philemon was intended, not just as personal instruction to him, but as a lesson for all the believers to learn and apply.

Philemon demonstrates the importance of how we treat others in light of the gospel. God expects us to be forgiving and merciful to others just as He has been to us. The commands Jesus taught are not just platitudes to be acknowledged or memorized; they are principles to be lived out with love and grace toward others. Relationships change in the light of the gospel.

"For this perhaps is why he was parted from you for a while, that you might have him back forever, no longer as a bondservant but more than a bondservant, as a beloved brother—especially to me, but how much more to you, both in the flesh and in the Lord."

PHILEMON 15-16

COLOSSIANS

Date: AD 61-62
Place of writing: Rome
Recipients: Christians in Colossae
Theme: Supremacy of Christ

Colossians was written by Paul during his first Roman imprisonment along with Ephesians, Philippians, and Philemon. Paul had been arrested for preaching the gospel and was awaiting trial before Caesar. Colossians is unique among these letters because Paul had never visited there (Col. 1:4) but had heard about their faith from Epaphras, who most likely founded the church (Col. 1:7). Epaphras may have learned of the gospel during Paul's two-year ministry in Ephesus, just one hundred miles west of Colossae.[32]

Gundry writes: "Under this hypothesis we can understand why Paul assumes authority over the Colossian church even though he has never been there: since he is a 'grandfather' of the church through his convert Epaphras, his judgment has been sought."[33] Epaphras is with Paul at the time of his writing of the letter and most likely brought him news of the church's health (Col. 4:12).

Paul wrote to refute heresies that had infiltrated the church confusing them. He commends their growing faith and then proclaims Christ as supreme over all the traditions and philosophies others were promoting. Because Jesus alone has reconciled them to God, He alone is worthy of their devotion.

In the first section, Paul greets the Colossians, calling them "saints and faithful brothers" (Col. 1:2). He then gives thanks for their faith and love that are bearing fruit and offers a prayer for their spiritual wisdom and endurance. The body of the letter begins with a hymn proclaiming the supremacy of Christ. Paul then declares their reconciliation to God through Christ's death and his suffering for their sake.

In chapter two, Paul affirms his care and concern for them and the church at Laodicea which was nearby and to whom he also sent a letter. Then, he encourages them to be established in the faith, not taken "captive by philosophy and empty deceit, according to human tradition," refuting the false

---

[32] Gundry, *A Survey of the NT,* 458.

[33] Ibid.

teachings of both Greek philosophy and Jewish traditions (Col. 2:8). He goes on to encourage them to put to death the sinful nature and walk as "God's chosen ones" with His Word in their hearts (Col. 3:12-17). He shares instructions for members of households that demonstrate godly behavior rather than cultural expectations of the day. Last, he closes with greetings from those with him in Rome and to those in Colossae and Laodicea, encouraging both churches to read both letters.

Colossians teaches us much about who Jesus is and who He calls us to be. Paul's hymn of Christ declared Him to be the image of the invisible God, the firstborn over all creation, Creator of all things, Sustainer of all things, preeminent over all things, the fullness of God, and the Reconciler of man to God.

Colossians also teaches us who we are in Him. We are reconciled, forgiven, filled with Him, alive in Christ, chosen, holy, and dearly loved. Colossians teaches us to keep our focus on Christ as we put to death the sinful nature and put on Christ's character of compassion, kindness, humility, gentleness, patience, forgiveness, and love.

· ·

"And you, who once were alienated and hostile in mind, doing evil deeds, he has now reconciled in his body of flesh by his death, in order to present you holy and blameless and above reproach before him."

COLOSSIANS 3:21-22

· ·

EPHESIANS

Date: AD 61-62
Place of writing: Rome
Recipients: Christians in Ephesus
Theme: The Gospel Changes Us

In another of the prison epistles, Paul wrote this letter to a community of believers he had spent about three years with (Acts 19). Paul preached the gospel and discipled the Christians in Ephesus, where both Jews and Gentiles made up the community of faith. He wrote, not to refute heresy or address concerns in the church, but rather to encourage and strengthen the faith of the believers there.

He began by reminding them of their spiritual blessings in Christ: they were chosen before the world began, set apart for Him, adopted as His children, and redeemed by the blood of Jesus. Having their sins forgiven, they were given wisdom and understanding of God's purpose—that they might believe in Him and be marked by the Holy Spirit as a guarantee of their inheritance in Christ.

Paul gave thanks for their faith and prayed they might continue to grow and understand the power of God available for those who trust in Him. Because of Christ's sacrifice, those who were once separated from God's promises (Gentiles) have now been reconciled and made one with Israel, together having access to God through His Spirit. Paul proclaimed the power of the gospel and prayed they might be rooted in God's love and able to understand that power at work within them.

He encouraged the Ephesians to live their lives in light of the gospel, humble, gentle, loving, seeking peace and unity in the Spirit. He called them to live as children of light, guarding their hearts against anger, unwholesome speech, sexual immorality, and deeds of darkness. Paul ends with instructions for relationships in Christ, such as husbands and wives, children and parents, and slaves and masters. These regulations did not condone slavery but stressed respect and dignity for one another amid the practices that already existed at that time.

Paul closed this letter with instructions for taking up the armor of God against the spiritual forces of evil at work in the world. He stressed prayer and the Word as the spiritual weapons for spiritual warfare.

Ephesians is a great encouragement to believers today to allow the power of the gospel to change who we are, what we believe about ourselves, and how we live in relationships with others. The gospel changes us, and Ephesians reminds us of that truth.

"For by grace you have been saved through faith. And this is not your own doing; it is the gift of God, not a result of works, so that no one may boast. For we are his workmanship, created in Christ Jesus for good works, which God prepared beforehand, that we should walk in them."

EPHESIANS 2:8-10

PHILIPPIANS

Date: AD 62
Place of writing: Rome
Recipients: Christians in Philippi
Theme: Joy in Christ

The last of the Prison Epistles, Philippians was written to the Christians in Philippi to thank them for their financial gift, to report on his circumstances, and to encourage them in the face of persecution to stand firm in their faith. Paul, Timothy, and Silas had visited there on their missionary journeys (Acts 16). During that time, they shared the gospel with Lydia, whose conversion led to the establishment of a local community of believers at her home. But Paul and Silas were also arrested and imprisoned in Philippi, where their praise while in chains led to a miraculous jailbreak and the conversion of the jailer and his household. This background is the context for the church community to whom Paul addressed this letter.

Paul wrote Philippians to encourage the believers in their financial partnership for the gospel and to pray for their spiritual growth. He reminded them that even though he was again imprisoned for preaching the gospel, his message was still being preached, and that was what mattered most. His use of the words joy or rejoice multiple times throughout this letter served to stir up the joy of the Philippians regardless of persecution and trials. He encouraged them to focus on Jesus and His humility and to shine like stars as they continued to share the hope of the gospel with others.

Last, Paul exhorted the Philippians to not be led astray by those Judaizers who still preached circumcision as necessary for salvation but to put their hope in what Christ had done in His crucifixion and resurrection. In one of the most powerful passages in his letters, Paul testified of his desire to know Christ, putting his past sins behind him and pressing on toward the goal of eternal life in Him. He reminded the believers that they can have joy and peace amid their circumstances as they keep their minds on things above.

This letter encourages us today to put our hope in Christ and His finished work on the cross, rejoicing in our future glory rather than dwelling on our past sins or present sufferings. Whether we have our physical needs met or we struggle with loss and need, we can be content in Christ because He meets all our spiritual needs, and that is enough.

"Therefore God has highly exalted him and bestowed on him the name that is above every name, so that at the name of Jesus every knee should bow, in heaven and on earth and under the earth, and every tongue confess that Jesus Christ is Lord, to the glory of God the Father."

PHILIPPIANS 2:9-11

1 & 2 TIMOTHY

Date: AD 63-64; 65
Place of writing: Macedonia; Rome
Recipients: Timothy (Ephesus)
Theme: Administration of churches; Timothy's commission

First and Second Timothy and Titus are called the Pastoral Letters because they are addressed not to churches but to individuals—Timothy and Titus. Timothy had been discipled by Paul and left to oversee the church in Ephesus. Paul considered Timothy his "true child in the faith" (1 Tim. 1:2) and shared these instructions so that Timothy could fulfill the call on his life.

In his first letter, Paul urged Timothy to put a stop to the false teaching going on in Ephesus and to contend for the gospel. Paul then gave Timothy instructions for order in the church gatherings and the administration of church offices so that these false teachings could be curtailed. He encouraged Timothy that the Spirit had shown him these kinds of teachings would occur, but his job as overseer was to point out their inconsistencies with the gospel. He also warned Timothy to carefully attend to his own life and doctrine, being diligent in the things of God.

Paul advised on relationships within the church and the administration of aid for widows so that no one is taken advantage of. The elders and deacons were expected to be men of integrity as well, and Timothy was charged to flee from any sin that would disrupt his ministry and to "pursue righteousness, godliness, faith, love, steadfastness, gentleness" (1 Tim. 6:11b). He encouraged Timothy to guard the gospel with which he had been entrusted, that it might be proclaimed in all its purity and truth.

Second Timothy was the last of Paul's letters, probably written from a second Roman imprisonment shortly before his death. Paul wrote to encourage Timothy to remain true to the faith instilled in him by his mother and grandmother. Even amid opposition and continued false teaching in the church at Ephesus, Timothy should put his hope in Jesus and endure hardship for the sake of the gospel, just as Paul had done.

He reminded Timothy to continue to study and teach the Word because it still had the power to change hearts and to correct the false teachers in the church. He encouraged Timothy to continue to grow his faith and gently instruct those who opposed him, knowing that godlessness would increase in the last days, but the gospel endures despite persecution. Last, he longed to see Timothy because many had deserted Paul in his final days, and he was lonely.

Both of these letters encourage us to live faithfully amid persecution and false teaching, while also contending for truth with gentleness and respect. God's Word still has the power to change hearts and lives, so knowing and standing on its truth is vital to the ministry of the gospel in every time and culture.

"Therefore do not be ashamed of the testimony about our Lord, nor of me his prisoner, but share in suffering for the gospel by the power of God, who saved us and called us to a holy calling, not because of our works but because of his own purpose and grace, which he gave us in Christ Jesus before the ages began, and which now has been manifested through the appearing of our Savior Christ Jesus, who abolished death and brought life and immortality to light through the gospel."

2 TIMOTHY 1:8-10

TITUS

Date: AD 63-64
Place of writing: Nicopolis
Recipients: Titus (Crete)
Theme: Administration of churches

The last of the Pastoral Epistles, the letter to Titus was also penned by Paul to one of his converts in Ephesus. Titus ministered with Paul in Corinth and later on the island of Crete, where Paul left him to oversee the church there. This letter likely was written between the writing of 1 and 2 Timothy.

Titus's role as an overseer was to appoint elders in the different churches on the island, so Paul reminded him of the qualifications for elders. He instructed Titus on what various leaders in the church should teach in accordance with sound doctrine, encouraging him to teach, encourage, and rebuke false teaching with authority.

Paul wrote that Titus should encourage the people to do what is good, not because their righteous deeds could save them but because they had been saved by Christ's mercy and justified by His grace. Therefore, they should devote themselves to God and what is good.

Titus encourages us today to be steadfast in both sharing and living out the gospel. Both our words and our witness should point to salvation that is found in Christ alone.

· ·

"But when the goodness and loving kindness of God our Savior appeared, he saved us, not because of works done by us in righteousness, but according to his own mercy, by the washing of regeneration and renewal of the Holy Spirit, whom he poured out on us richly through Jesus Christ our Savior."

TITUS 3:4-6

· ·

The General Epistles

Faith

THE GENERAL

Epistles

The general epistles are the remaining letters of the New Testament that do not have Paul as their confirmed author. Hebrews, in particular, remains anonymous to us today. The other letters have their authors identified as James, Peter, Jude, and John.

The term *catholic*, which means "general" or "universal," has been used to identify these eight NT books. Hebrews is titled after its audience, but the remaining seven are titled according to their authors, much like the Gospels.[34]

Like the Pauline epistles, these letters should be read straight through without removing passages or verses from their immediate literary, historical, or cultural contexts. These letters give us divinely inspired insight into how the early church lived out the principles of Christianity during persecution from Judaism and the Roman Empire. They contain powerful theological truths that can be applied in our current context today.

---

[34] Gundry, *A Survey of the NT,* 516.

JAMES

Author: James, Half-brother of Jesus
Date: AD 40s or 50s
Place of writing: Jerusalem
Recipients: Jewish Christians of the Dispersion
Theme: Christian conduct

Written by James, half-brother of Jesus and the leader of the church at Jerusalem, James is a practical manual of Christian conduct. Written in a style similar to Proverbs and highlighting many of the principles Jesus taught in the Sermon on the Mount, James encouraged Jewish believers scattered throughout the empire to live faithfully for Jesus.

Having been martyred in 62, James wrote the letter before that date, but it could have been penned much earlier since the Jerusalem Council (Acts 15) that took place in the 50s is not mentioned. It has a distinctly Jewish "flavor" that may be due to its early writing when most believers were Jewish converts.

James encouraged Christians to rejoice in trials and tests because they produce perseverance and spiritual growth toward maturity. He stressed the importance of seeking godly wisdom rather than worldly wealth and being doers of the Word. While some pit James's instruction about faith and works against Paul's treatise about faith and grace (Romans and Galatians), the two are not opposed but rather two sides of the same coin. Paul wrote to correct an overemphasis on works; James wrote to correct an overemphasis on faith. Both of them agree that justification (being made right with God) is by grace through faith and that faith is demonstrated by good works.

James addressed self-control with the tongue, which can cause great damage. He discussed godly wisdom and worldly wisdom, encouraging believers to seek the wisdom of God. James attributed disputes among believers as evidence of friendship with the world and instructed believers to humbly submit to God and resist the world and the devil. He warned those who oppress others that they would be held accountable for their actions.

James ended his letter with a call to be patient under suffering and to stand firm, trusting God to be near with compassion and mercy. He encouraged them to pray in times of trouble, to praise in good times, and to confess their sins to God.

James is a great encouragement to us today to check our hearts, seek God's wisdom, and live our lives submitted to God and His ways. His practical wisdom for everyday life can help us to keep our hearts in check and aligned with God's Word.

"But the wisdom from above is first pure, then peaceable, gentle, open to reason, full of mercy and good fruits, impartial and sincere. And a harvest of righteousness is sown in peace by those who make peace."

JAMES 3:17-18

JUDE

Author: Jude, half-brother of Jesus
Date: AD 60s
Place of writing: Unknown
Recipients: Christians everywhere
Theme: Warnings against false teaching

Jude was the brother of James and half-brother of Jesus. He wrote this short letter to Christians but does not specify a location. The date is also unknown, but because of similarities to parts of 2 Peter, it is generally dated within the same period, probably the mid-60s.

Jude planned to write to them about their salvation but felt compelled to instead urge them to contend for the faith amid false teaching. He wrote of the godless men among them who assumed that salvation by grace gave them a license to sin. Jude rebuked their unbelief in Jesus as Lord. He reminded them that the same God judged sin in the Old Testament, and he still judges sin. Faith in Christ gives us power over sin to live a new life.

He referenced several OT examples, as well as quotes from the Assumption of Moses and the book of Enoch. These writings are not part of our OT canon, but they were respected ancient Jewish writings that Jews would have been familiar with. Jude's purpose was to remind the believers that these men who had infiltrated the church with false teaching were rebellious, ungodly, and would face judgment.

He then encouraged the believers to persevere during such teaching and to build themselves up in the faith, praying in the Spirit. He instructed them to be merciful to those who doubt and to rescue those headed for destruction. Jude reminded the believers that Jesus was able to keep them and to present them to the Father "without fault and with great joy" (24).

Jude encourages us today to recognize false teaching, share the gospel truth with others, and be merciful toward those who doubt. We should not view grace as a license to sin but as the power not to sin. The gospel truth teaches us that through Christ we die to sin and we are raised in Him to live a new life. Jude reminds us to contend for that truth.

"But you, beloved, building yourselves up in your most holy faith and praying in the Holy Spirit, keep yourselves in the love of God, waiting for the mercy of our Lord Jesus Christ that leads to eternal life."

JUDE 20-21

1 AND 2 PETER

Author: Peter
Date: AD 63-64; 65
Place of writing: Rome
Recipients: Christians in Asia Minor
Theme: Conduct of suffering Christians; Christian belief

The Petrine Epistles—letters of Peter—were both penned by the Apostle Peter in the mid-60s before his martyrdom sometime between 65 and 68. They were most likely written from Rome to Christians throughout Asia Minor. These Christians (both Jews and Gentiles) were suffering persecution that had scattered them throughout the empire. The Gospels and Acts provide the context for Peter's life and ministry.

Peter wrote his first letter to address the living hope the believers had in Christ. That hope enabled them to rejoice even in their trials because their genuine faith would result in salvation. He encouraged them to live holy lives in light of that hope, loving each other, ridding themselves of sin, and growing in their salvation.

Peter described them as a chosen people belonging to God who had rescued them from the darkness of sin and brought them into the light of life. He called them to live good lives so others would see their good works and glorify God. He gave instructions for submission to authority, relationships in marriage, and being prepared to give an answer for their hope in Christ. Peter acknowledged their suffering for Christ as something to be expected.

In his second letter, written shortly before his martyrdom, Peter reminded them of the historical reliability of their Christian faith based on eyewitness testimony. This second letter addressed issues of false teaching within the church. Peter reminded the believers that God had given them everything they needed to live a godly life. He called them to right living as a result of right doctrine. Peter confirmed the divine inspiration of Scripture as the basis of that doctrine.

Peter's letters remind us of what our behavior in a non-Christian society should look like. They encourage us to rejoice when our faith is challenged and to be ready to share the gospel when people ask the reason for our hope. By imitating Christ and His character, believers can expose the injustice of persecution and point people to the cross.

······································

"For to this you have been called, because Christ also suffered for you, leaving you an example, so that you might follow in his steps."

1 PETER 2:21

······································

HEBREWS

Author: Unknown
Date: AD 60s
Place of writing: Unknown
Recipients: Jewish Christians in Rome
Theme: Superiority of Christ

The letter to the Hebrews stands out in the NT canon for several reasons: (1) The author remains anonymous; (2) It is a letter with a closing but no greeting; (3) It is not addressed to any specific audience; (4) It is written more like a sermon than a letter; (5) It is very Jewish in nature.

Hebrews was most likely written to a Jewish audience facing immense persecution. The letter was an encouragement to persevere and not turn back to Judaism because Jesus is greater than the angels, Moses, the priesthood, the High Priest, the covenant, the sanctuary, and the sacrifices. The old Jewish system had been superseded by the priesthood of Christ through His once-for-all sacrifice for sins. The writer reminded these Jewish Christians that all of the OT practices pointed to Jesus, the ultimate fulfillment and the greater One whose sacrifice, intercession, and covenant made all the old obsolete.

Animal sacrifices could temporarily atone for sin but had to be repeated. The high priest could make sacrifices for the people, but he was a sinner too. The old covenant was good, but it was not sufficient. The writer of Hebrews exhorted the believers to not turn back to Judaism under intense persecution because God's revelation in Christ was far superior to the old covenant based on the law.

Hebrews highlights faith as the basis of the Christian life. He defines faith, then describes the lives of faithful men and women of the past. He uses their faith as an example to the persecuted believers to endure to the end. If those heroes of faith could endure having not seen the reality of their hope which was Jesus—how much more should his audience hold fast to their hope in the resurrected Christ?

Hebrews reminds us to run our race with faith and perseverance because our eyes are on Jesus who endured much suffering for us. By following His example, we too can endure with faith in the hope that is set before us.

"Therefore, since we are surrounded by so great a cloud of witnesses, let us also lay aside every weight, and sin which clings so closely, and let us run with endurance the race that is set before us, looking to Jesus, the founder and perfecter of our faith, who for the joy that was set before him endured the cross, despising the shame, and is seated at the right hand of the throne of God."

HEBREWS 12:1-2

1, 2, AND 3 JOHN

Author: John
Date: AD late 80s or early 90s
Place of writing: Ephesus
Recipients: Christians in and around Ephesus; Gaius (3 John)
Themes: Christian faith and practice; Christian love and truth; commendation and warning

Called the Johannine Epistles, these three short letters were written by the Apostle John, the "beloved disciple" and author of the Gospel of John and the Revelation. They were most likely written near the end of the first century to Christians in Asia Minor and the area surrounding Ephesus.

Continuing with his Gospel emphasis on the Word, light and darkness, love, and the world, John wrote to proclaim the truth amid heresy. Gnosticism, which was a heresy of the late first and second centuries, taught that the spirit is good but all matter is evil, including man's body. They, therefore, denied the humanity of Christ since a physical body would have been evil. Gnostics believed salvation was not by faith but by special knowledge (gnosis). They thought it was okay to sin since matter was the source of evil, not laws.

John refuted these false teachings and proclaimed that the measure of genuine Christianity was right living, love for others, and belief in Jesus as the incarnate Christ. He focused on love for Christ and not the world, encouraging believers to test the spirits because of the many false prophets. He reminded them that their faith in the greater One would give them confidence in their hope of eternal life.

John's second letter was written near the end of his life to an unknown church. It is a call to Christian love, another warning against false teachers, and an encouragement to use discernment in evaluating the teachings of those who claim to be Christians. This short letter focuses on truth and love.

John's third letter was addressed to Gaius, a Christian in one of the provinces of Asia and a friend who lived in a region around Ephesus. He commended Gaius who was faithful and walked in truth. But John warned a man named Diotrophes who was rejecting teachers of the faith. Again, John stressed discernment in recognizing truth and error. It was a call to imitate what is good and reject what is evil. Demetrius was another brother who was commended by John for speaking the truth.

These three letters have a common theme of being able to know, discern, and agree with truth while recognizing and rejecting what is not. They remind us today that we also are surrounded by false teaching and cultural deception. We must be wise and discerning, measuring everything against the truth of Scripture, so that we are not led astray.

"And this is the testimony, that God gave us eternal life, and this life is in his Son. Whoever has the Son has life; whoever does not have the Son of God does not have life."

1 JOHN 5:11-12

The Revelation

Restoration

THE Revelation

Revelation is the literal rendering of the Greek *Apocalypse* which means "uncovering or unveiling."[35] The book of Revelation is usually either considered scary and avoided or becomes a source of obsession about end-time events. I suggest it should not be approached in either of these ways but rather as what it was intended—an encouragement to persevere because Jesus will return and restore all things and bring perfect righteousness and justice to all the world.

Revelation was written by the Apostle John, who had been exiled to the island of Patmos, around AD 95 under the persecution of the Roman emperor Domitian. He had been exiled there for his faith as an old man, probably in his late 80s by this time. This is the same John, one of the original twelve apostles, who also wrote the Gospel of John, and 1, 2, and 3 John. He is the only apostle believed to have survived martyrdom and died a natural death.

Revelation is the only book in the Bible that promises blessings to those who read it, hear it, and take it to heart (1:3). While the genre (actually a combination of three genres: epistle, apocalyptic, and prophetic) makes it somewhat difficult to read and interpret, a few principles for understanding this type of language can be helpful. We have already discussed epistles, which the first portion of Revelation includes in its messages to the seven churches. So, let's look at these other two genres.

---

[35] Gundry, *A Survey of NT,* 548.

CHARACTERISTICS OF PROPHETIC AND APOCALYPTIC LANGUAGE

PROPHETIC	APOCALYPTIC
Word from the Lord	Vision from the Lord
Announcing judgment	Describing events to come
God's control over history	God's control over the future
Calls for an audience response	Describes future regardless of response
Less visual and symbolic	More visual and symbolic

How do we interpret the symbolic language?

- Some of it, John tells us: Stars=angels, lampstands=churches

- Much of it is interpreted in light of the context of the rest of the Bible

- Jesus is the Lamb (Reminders of the Passover in Exodus, atonement sacrifice of tabernacle/temple worship)

- Beast throughout Scripture represents a spiritual power that empowers earthly empires (see Daniel)

- Babylon represents those earthly kingdoms of the world that put faith in military and economic power rather than God and who rebel against God—at the time of the writing that would have been the Roman Empire

- Use of the number 7=completeness (Genesis)

- Series of 3 cycles of judgment: 7 seals, 7 trumpets, and 7 bowls remind us of the flood, plagues, exile, and times of God's judgment for the darkness and sin in the world

We have to read Revelation in light of the whole Bible beginning with the cycle of sin and judgment in Genesis, through the sacrificial worship system of Exodus and Leviticus, and in light of the prophecies of Daniel.

Just as the chaos before creation in Genesis was overcome when God created light, Jesus' life, death, and resurrection brought light and hope to the darkness of our world as He defeated evil on the cross by His death. Revelation is about the victory of Jesus' triumph over sin and darkness and the reuniting of heaven and earth as intended in Eden.

There are many interpretations of the timing of end-time events. Which events are past, present, and future? What is the timing of Christ's return, the final battle, the thousand-year reign, and the New Jerusalem? Most of these questions cannot be answered with certainty and don't seem to be the primary purpose of the book.

A better way to interpret Revelation is to ask: What was John's purpose to his readers in the historical context in which it was written?

John wanted to provide hope, to challenge them to resist the demands of emperor worship, to know that they would be persecuted, but that there would be a final showdown between Jesus and Satan. Jesus would be victorious, and they would be vindicated and rewarded for their faithfulness. That is the same message for us today.

> *"And I heard a loud voice from the throne saying, 'Now the dwelling of God is with men, and he will live with them. They will be his people, and God himself will be with them and be their God'" (21:3).*

From the Garden to the Tabernacle to the cross, God has desired to dwell with His people. Our sin, darkness, and rebellion separated us from His holiness; Jesus atoned for our sins, the Holy Spirit indwells us and our bodies become His temple. One day we will be with Him forever. Genesis starts with the River and the Tree of Life and Revelation ends with them both; Eden is restored.

For the persecuted church then and for us now, our hope is in His return for His bride when He will deal with evil and we will dwell forever with Him.

> *"Behold, I am coming soon! My reward is with me, and I will give to everyone according to what he has done" (22:12).*

It's a beautiful promise for believers to hold onto their faith and trust Jesus to make all things new.

Don't be afraid to read it or caught up trying to interpret the timing of end-time events; instead, be encouraged that we serve the God who alone is worthy to receive power and wealth and wisdom and strength and honor and glory and praise!

To the One who was and is and is to come, be all the glory! Amen.

Gather

In this first step, we want to gather information about the background of the book. This will help to situate the book in its original context and avoid misreading.

- Who wrote it?

- What do you know about the author?

- To whom were they writing?

- What were the basic time and historical events surrounding it?

- What was the author's purpose to the original audience?

- What was the culture like?

- What is the genre of the book?

- What do you know about this particular genre?

- Where does this book fit into the overall message of the Bible?

Read

Next, we want to read the book straight through from beginning to end without marking or taking notes. Read the passage a few times in different translations, if possible.

Observe

Mark or jot down any keywords, repeated words or phrases, and any lists or comparisons. Take note of any questions you have. At this stage, you just want to ask, "What does it say?" You are looking for the plain meaning of the passage in its context. Try not to approach the Word with preconceived ideas about what the passage says but with fresh eyes to observe it in its own time and culture.

Wait

Don't try to find answers to all your questions yet. Don't look at study notes or consult commentaries or cross-references. Just sit with the text itself and soak it in.

Think

Now you want to seek to understand what the text means. What did the author intend to communicate to the original audience? Your study Bible will include cross-references for consideration. These are other passages in the Bible that give further information related to the passage you are studying. Always let Scripture interpret Scripture. Then summarize the passage in your own words, taking note of how the passage fits into God's bigger story, the metanarrative of Scripture (creation, the fall, redemption, and restoration).

Ask the following questions:

- What does it tell me about God and His character?
- What does it tell me about people in general?

Hold

Last, you want to hold to God's truths for your own life through application. Ask the following questions:

- Is there a truth I need to apply?
- A sin to confess?
- A promise to believe?
- A command to follow?
- How does it apply to the church in general?
- How does God want me to respond?
- What practical steps can I take to apply what I have learned?

RESOURCES ON THE
Cultural Context
OF THE BIBLE

Bailey, Kenneth. *Jesus through Middle Eastern Eyes: Cultural Studies in the Gospels.* Downers Grove: IVP Academic, 2008.

McLelland, Kristi. *Jesus and Women: In the First Century and Now.* Nashville: Lifeway Press, 2022.

Richards, E. Randolph, and Brandon J. O'Brien. *Misreading Scripture with Western Eyes: Removing Cultural Blinders to Better Understand the Bible.* Downers Grove: IVP Books, 2012.

Spangler, Ann, and Lois Tverberg. *Sitting at the Feet of Rabbi Jesus: How the Jewishness of Jesus Can Transform Your Faith.* Grand Rapids: Zondervan, 2018.

Tverberg, Lois. *Reading the Bible with Rabbi Jesus: How a Jewish Perspective Can Transform Your Understanding.* Grand Rapids: Baker Books, 2017.

_____. *Walking in the Dust of Rabbi Jesus: How the Jewish Words of Jesus Can Change Your Life.* Grand Rapids: Zondervan, 2012.

HOW TO HAVE New Life

Do you want to know how to have new life?

We were each created by God to know and worship Him. God loves you and desires a personal relationship with you.

The Bible teaches us that we are all sinners. Romans 3:23 says, "For all have sinned and fall short of the glory of God." God is holy and righteous and good. He created the world and all that is in it. But we are all born with a sinful nature because He made us with a free will—the opportunity to choose whether or not we will follow Him. Left to ourselves, we will fall short of His glory and righteousness. This sin separates us from God and leads only to death. Romans 6:23 says, "For the wages of sin is death."

But because God loves us so much, He made a way for us to know Him through His Son. "But God demonstrates his own love for us in this: while we were still sinners, Christ died for us" (Romans 5:8). God sent His only Son, Jesus, who lived a perfect life, to die on the cross for us as payment for our sins. He took the punishment on Himself so that we could be free from sin's penalty.

The rest of Romans 6:23 (above) says this: "But the gift of God is eternal life in Christ Jesus." We are sinners, and yet through Jesus and the gift of God, we can have eternal life. The truth is that we really can have a personal relationship with God through His Son, Jesus.

So what do you do to be saved?

Romans 10:9-10 tells us "That if you confess with your mouth, 'Jesus is Lord,' and believe in your heart that God raised him from the dead, you will be saved. For it is with your heart that you believe and are justified, and it is with your mouth that you confess and are saved."

If God is speaking to your heart right now and you want to be saved, pray a prayer like this one:

Lord God,

I believe that You are God and that You created me to know You. I believe that You sent Your Son to die on the cross for my sins and that He rose again and lives forever. I know that I am a sinner and I confess my sins to You now. I ask You to forgive me and cleanse me and come to live inside my heart and be the Lord of my life. I choose to follow You and live for You from this day forward.

In Jesus' name,

Amen

If you just prayed a prayer like this one, please let me know the good news. Find a Bible-believing Christian church and begin to read the Bible and talk to God every day. You've just begun your new life in Him. Congratulations! Your life will never be the same!

GET GROUNDED AND
Keep Growing

You want to study the Bible and grow your faith. I know you do. And I know you want to start each day with a habit of spending time with Jesus. I also know that even when your heart is right, life can often get in the way.

Groceries must be shopped, laundry folded, homework checked, meals prepared, work done, relationships built, ministry carried out. And even when we have the best of intentions, it's really hard to stay consistent with in-depth Bible study.

But when we don't stay in the Word, we don't grow. Relationships are harder, work suffers, real ministry is impossible, and our hearts grow discontent. That's because apart from HIM we can do nothing. And His Word is the truth we need to walk in day by day.

The good news is that it doesn't have to be that way. You don't have to just settle for the crumbs from the Master's table. That's a lie from the enemy. Instead, you can sit down and feast on His Word. Even if you are super busy.

Grounded and Growing is a ministry dedicated to encouraging your spiritual growth through practical strategies and helpful resources for serious Bible study that transforms lives. Just scan the code below for more resources.

- Books and Bible studies
- Anatomy of the Bible course
- The FOCUSED 15 Challenge
- Private Facebook group, *Growing Your Faith*
- Devotional Blog
- Quiet Time Guide
- Speaking Events

ABOUT THE
Author

Jennifer Hayes Yates is a wife, mama, writer, and speaker with an empty nest and a Southern accent. Having taught in Christian education for twenty-two years, she has a passion for communicating God's truth and inspiring busy women to grow their faith one quiet moment with Jesus at a time.

Jennifer is now a blogger, best-selling author, and passionate speaker. Lover of all things Jesus, books, and coffee, she can be found in quiet corners or busy spaces, sipping lattes, studying commentaries, and chatting up strangers.

But she's still just a small-town girl hoping to glorify God in all she writes and make a few disciples along the way.

You can follow Jennifer on Facebook, Instagram, and at Jenniferhyates.com.

Thank you so much for reading and studying God's Word with me.

My heart is for you to get to know Jesus better through serious study of the Bible. I pray this resource has been a catalyst toward that end.

I would love your feedback. If *Get Grounded* has been a blessing to you, would you consider leaving a helpful review on Amazon? It would mean so much to me and help me as I plan future books and resources.

Thank you and may God richly bless you as you grow your faith in Him.

Jennifer

Bibliography

Aucker, W. Brian. "Joel." In *The ESV Women's Study Bible*. Edited by Wayne Grudem. Wheaton, IL: Crossway, 2020.

Barker, Kenneth, General Editor, *The NIV Study Bible*. Grand Rapids: Zondervan, 1984.

Barker, Kenneth L., and John R. Kohlenberger. *1, 2 Kings. Expositor's Bible Commentary, Abridged Edition: Old Testament*. Grand Rapids: Zondervan, 2017.

Block, Daniel Isaac. *Judges, Ruth*. vol. 6, *The New American Commentary*. Nashville: Broadman & Holman Publishers, 1999.

Downs, Bert. *Bible Survey: A Big Screen Perspective*, BiblicalTraining.org, 2020.

Duvall, J. Scott, and J. Daniel Hays. *Grasping God's Word: A Hands-On Approach to Reading, Interpreting, and Applying the Bible*, 4th ed. Grand Rapids: Zondervan Academic, 2020.

Estes, Daniel J. *Handbook on the Wisdom Books and Psalms*. Grand Rapids: Baker Academic, 2005.

Fee, Gordon D., and Douglas Stuart. *How to Read the Bible for All Its Worth*, 4th ed. Grand Rapids: Zondervan, 2014.

Gundry, Robert H. *A Survey of the New Testament*, 5th ed. Grand Rapids: Zondervan, 2012.

Guthrie, George H. *Read the Bible for Life: Your Guide to Understanding & Living God's Word*. Nashville: B&H Publishing, 2011.

Hamilton, Victor P. *Handbook on the Historical Books*. Grand Rapids: Baker Publishing Group, 2001.

Hays, J. Daniel. "Reading the Old Testament Laws" In *Read the Bible for Life: Your Guide to Understanding and Living God's Word, edited by George H. Guthrie, 95-110. Nashville: B&H Publishing, 2011.*

Klein, William W., Craig L. Blomberg, and Robert L. Hubbard, Jr. *Introduction to Biblical Interpretation*, 3rd. ed. Grand Rapids: Zondervan, 2017.

Mears, Henrietta. *What the Bible Is All About*. 2nd rev. ed. Ventura, CA: Regal Books, 1997.

Stacy, Robert Wayne. Video Lecture for NBST 515. Liberty University, Lynchburg, VA, 2019.

Strauss, Mark L. *Four Portraits, One Jesus: A Survey of Jesus and the Gospels*. Grand Rapids: Zondervan, 2007.

Made in the USA
Middletown, DE
11 August 2024

58542507R00113